Diving
FOR
Starfish

ALSO BY CHERIE BURNS

Searching for Beauty:
The Life of Millicent Rogers, the American Heiress
Who Taught the World About Style

The Great Hurricane: 1938

Stepmotherhood:
How to Survive Without Feeling Frustrated,
Left Out, or Wicked

Diving
FOR
Starfish

THE JEWELER, THE ACTRESS, THE HEIRESS,
AND ONE OF THE WORLD'S
MOST ALLURING PIECES OF JEWELRY

Cherie Burns

ST. MARTIN'S PRESS ⚐ NEW YORK

www.stmartins.com

Designed by Devan Norman

The Library of Congress Cataloging-in-Publication Data is available upon request.

ISBN 978-1-250-05620-7 (hardcover)
ISBN 978-1-4668-5981-4 (ebook)

Our books may be purchased in bulk for promotional, educational, or business use. Please contact your local bookseller or the Macmillan Corporate and Premium Sales Department at 1-800-221-7945, extension 5442, or by email at MacmillanSpecialMarkets@macmillan.com.

First Edition: March 2018

10   9   8   7   6   5   4   3   2   1

In memory of my mother, Betty, who had a certain flair

Objects have always been carried, sold, bartered, stolen, retrieved and lost. People have always given gifts. It is how you tell their stories that matters.

—Edmund de Waal, *The Hare with Amber Eyes:*
A Family's Century of Art and Loss

Diving
FOR
Starfish

Chapter One

As I imagine it, a pearlescent moon rose over the mansard rooftops of Paris in the soft dusk as the streets of the First Arrondissement emptied below. Upstairs, inside a building festooned with wrought-iron balconies, sat a frail plain-faced woman sketching at her desk in a cramped atelier. Beside her sketchpad was a small collection of seashells. Some still held bits of dried seaweed and a few grains of sand in their bleached creases. Improbably (remember, I am imagining) a pungent whiff of salt spray, evoking the far-off beaches of Brittany, puffed through a window above her desk and swirled around the room. Filled with a sudden inspiration, Juliette Moutard drew a piece of jewelry in the form of a hand-sized starfish. It was a lush and throbbing likeness, rich and yet natural; an evocation of the primal sea bottom. With her paint set she colored in red rubies and purple amethysts along the ripples of its features. In my mind's eye the rays undulated and the stones flung sparks into the moonlight.

*   *   *

Moments of real inspiration are hard to know and often more pedestrian than we imagine, but this starfish deserves a fairy-tale introduction. I can't bear thinking it had been drawn on a cocktail napkin. The unembellished fact is that in one electrifying stroke, a design that would haunt and charm jewelry aficionados for the next eighty years took shape on Moutard's sketchpad. Her employer, the exacting Paris jewelry salon owner Jeanne Boivin, had urged Moutard to consider sea creatures in her designs. Europe was full of rich women, many of them Americans with newfound fortunes, flaunting their wealth and looking for innovative jewelry that would make a bold statement. Madame Boivin often brought seashells and crustaceans from the beaches of Brittany, which she knew from her childhood, and left them in the workshop of the Boivin salon.

One of the most captivating and enduring pieces of jewelry would emerge from Moutard's drawing and crawl into the world of collectors and jewelers to enchant and confound them for the next eighty years. The untraditional pairing of lush purple and red stones, the miraculous articulation that mimicked life, and the legend of the Paris salon where it took form were part of its intrigue. That *étoile de mer*, with its 71 cabochon rubies and 241 small amethysts, had five rays, two of them flipped slightly at the ends, flowing out from a center mound adorned with one large ruby. Astonishingly, its rays were articulated so they could curl and conform to the bustline or shoulders of the women who wore it. It moved. A sigh, a breath, a burst of laughter would cause small shifts of its bejeweled form.

Moutard, and Boivin, as well as the movie star and the beautiful heiress who bought the first two versions of Juliette's creation have long since vanished into eternity. But the Boivin starfish live on, casting their red and purple glow on a string of rarefied owners.

The older they become, the more they are sought after. Moutard could not have known how long these brooches would continue to bewitch jewelry aficionados in Europe and America, or how many hands they would pass through from 1936 until the present. She could not have known the lives and stories they would intersect or the drama, intrigue, and deception that would sometimes surround them. All that was for me to discover.

Chapter Two

KNEW NONE OF THIS, AND WOULDN'T HAVE CARED MUCH IF I had, when I strolled down Fifth Avenue one gentle September evening eight decades later. The leaves on the trees in Central Park hadn't fallen yet and the buzz of Fashion Week, ongoing in the city, filled the streets. Fall, when the dusk drags on until the lights in the hotels and department store windows begin to glow, is always my favorite season in Manhattan. I walked slowly in high heels in the twilight, savoring the moment.

I was headed to a party for a book I had written, hosted by the exclusive jeweler Verdura. The guest list was an impressive mix of social and celebrated names. I entered the airy marble lobby of the building on Fifth Avenue off the corner of Fifty-sixth Street and walked past the black grand piano in front of the reception desk. On the eleventh floor a silver-carpeted hallway led toward

Verdura's door. I had been there before while reporting on my subject, the heiress Millicent Rogers. She had bought jewels from Verdura.

That night the salon was even more magical than usual. I had never been in Verdura after dark. The showrooms fill a corner looking down into Central Park. The lights of Bergdorf Goodman across the street had begun to sparkle. Large photos of Coco Chanel and the elegant Italian Count Fulco di Verdura, the salon's founder and namesake, hung in their places on the espresso-brown reception room walls. Other photos, of Liz Taylor and Richard Burton, Greta Garbo, and Babe Paley, all Verdura clients, were arranged around the rooms, enveloped in a golden glow as the sun finally set.

Verdura is one of those jewelry salons too exclusive to have an entrance on the street, as Tiffany and Cartier do down below. It does not cater to "passing trade." Rather, its clientele shops mostly by appointment. That night a refined calm filled the minutes before the party began. The plush off-white carpet muffled most sounds and two small but opulent front salons stood nearly empty, patrolled by two square-jawed men in tweed sports jackets. In my party mood, I spoke cheerily to them, thinking they were early guests or Verdura staff until I realized from their awkward reserve and reluctance to take their eyes off the doorway that they were security, there to protect the jewelry that was displayed in glass showcases. Diamond cluster ear clips, curb-link gold bracelets, Verdura's signature Maltese crosses, hinged stone cuffs, and an array of original designs once sported by Diana Vreeland, Marlene Dietrich, and Greta Garbo, to name a few—they all needed watching during the party.

Ward Landrigan, the owner of Verdura, greeted me. He is a well-dressed man of medium height with a shock of silver hair and an open smile. Associates who admire his sales skills say he can talk a suicide jumper off a ledge. His assured hand gestures give him an air of insouciance when he is speaking. On an earlier visit he had told me how in his salad days in the jewelry business he had been required by an insurer to keep Richard Burton, and the Krupp diamond he was delivering to him for Elizabeth Taylor, in sight until Burton's insurance coverage went into effect. For nearly a week he stayed in the Dorchester Hotel in London where Burton and Taylor slept while Burton was filming *Where Eagles Dare.* He'd had many tales to tell and a fine appreciation for people and jewelry. Now, he enthusiastically steered me toward the back salon, where a treat was in store.

I'd been told that I, along with Verdura's female staff and the party's cohostess, would be dressed in Verdura jewels for the evening. "Look around and pick out what you like," Ward told me. With a wave of his hand, much like a fairy godmother with a magic wand (or Merlin in this instance), he indicated the jewelry exhibited in the cases around the salon's showrooms. Instantly, I was a kid in the candy store. Choosing was difficult. Ward's elegant assistant, Betty, jumped in to make me feel at ease. We surveyed several options. "Here, try these," she said, handing me a smashing pair of turquoise and diamond earrings the size of chestnuts with a matching ring and bracelet. I tried them on a bit dutifully, then looked at myself in the mirror and saw how well they went with my tan and my navy blue dress. I decided to wear them for the party, which was about to begin.

A server brought me a glass of champagne. Ward appeared again and took my elbow. He was excited. "Come, let me show you something," he said, leading me to a large glass showcase sitting in the middle of the salon's gallery. There, prominently displayed on a gray velvet pillowed pedestal, was a golden starfish the size of my palm, with rubies and amethysts cascading down its ridged rays. Its articulated arms were fully extended, and under the showroom lighting it seemed not just to sparkle, but also to effervesce as if it were visibly radioactive.

The starfish looked real enough to climb out of the case and march up my arm. I was off balance for a moment. I understood that I should know something about it. What was its importance? There was something familiar about it but I couldn't remember what. Proudly, Ward explained it had belonged to Millicent Rogers, the subject of my biography. He unlocked the glass case. "Would you like to hold it?" he asked.

I hesitated, my eyes locked on the brooch. It was intimidating and gorgeous. The etiquette of touching such a valuable, large piece of jewelry seemed unclear to me. Would my fingers smudge it? Its purple and red stones throbbed under the bright showroom lights. I almost wondered if it would feel hot. As a reporter I had experienced this kind of moment before, brushing up against glamorous and wealthy worlds and the people who inhabit them, briefly sharing in that universe, playing along. But this opulent work of art upset my game.

When I came back to myself, I made a mistake, one I would regret many times over. Without clearly knowing why, I demurred. It was enough to see the brooch. I didn't need to hold it, I explained almost apologetically. Frankly, I was distracted by the excitement and anticipation of being the center of attention, along with my book, at this party. It was about to begin. Guests were coming through the doorway. We moved on and greeted them in the entry salon.

For the next several hours I was in the swirl of a dizzying array of people. It was my Author's Moment, which I had found are rare and to be savored. I watched the Russian model Tatiana Surroko write a six-figure check for a Maltese-cross bracelet. The old friends I had invited arrived. I posed with the star of a TV series, with Ward, and later with my adult children. I signed books and smiled, chatted with the few reporters covering the event, and then the party was over. There had been no chance to revisit the brooch. A bit like Cinderella, I turned in my Verdura jewelry and replaced it with my own. Then I changed my shoes and walked out into the night for dinner with family and friends. Only recently have I realized that I must have been trailed out the door by a faint whiff of pungent sea spray.

Chapter Three

THE NEXT DAY I RETURNED TO THANK THE VERDURA staff for the party. It was business as usual in the salon, and Ward, summoned from the office in back, came out to see me. I asked if I could look again at the starfish. It was gone, he told me. *Gone?* My first thought was that someone at the party the night before had bought it. "Where did it come from?" I asked. "Oh, I don't know," Ward said breezily, brushing the question aside. I thought he mumbled that his son and partner Nico had gotten it, but in the same beat he directed me to the front salon, where there was some excitement about a new eye-catching piece from the estate of Liz Taylor that he thought I might want to see. For the moment I forgot about the starfish, but before leaving I asked again, a little wistfully, where it had gone.

"A jeweler in London, I think," he said before he waved good-bye and jauntily retreated down the hall to his office.

I was startled that the starfish had disappeared so quickly. Obviously, it had arrived as an honored guest just for the party. I didn't know then that fine jewelry like the brooch can move at lightning speed in the hands of dealers who want to expose it as widely as possible. And I was only beginning to suspect that for the next several years I would look back with real regret that I had missed the chance to hold one of Juliette Moutard's ruby and amethyst starfish.

Soon after the Verdura party I was invited to the salon of another jeweler in New York, Siegelson. I had never heard of Siegelson, which will suggest to jewelry aficionados how little I knew about the fine-jewelry business. I wasn't even sure why Sarah Davis, the staffer who invited me to visit the office on Forty-ninth and Fifth, wanted to see me, except that it had something to do with Millicent Rogers's jewelry collection. She told me that she had Rogers's ruby heart brooch that had been created by the designer Paul Flato, probably the most famous American jeweler in history. They'd love to show it to me. She said that she and Lee Siegelson liked my book. I was flattered.

On my way to Siegelson I marveled that although I had lived in Manhattan for over twenty-five years and peeked into various worlds as a reporter, I'd never brushed up against this hidden world of fine jewelry, salons tucked into high floors above Fifth Avenue. I had shopped for a diamond pendant for our daughter in the diamond district, had looked for a pearl necklace at Mikimoto and Fortunoff, and trafficked in and out of Tiffany for presents and a punch bowl over the years, but I had never stepped behind the curtain of the new world that was inviting me in now.

Siegelson's waiting room was a notch less posh and a touch more corporate than Verdura's chocolate-brown salon up the avenue, but the muted gray walls and sculpted bronze busts that decorated the waiting room created an equally rarefied air. Sarah Davis greeted me warmly. I noticed that my book with its pale turquoise cover was positioned centrally on a bookshelf at the end of the hallway to the spacious office where I was led.

Lee Siegelson, the forty-six-year-old principal in the business, soon appeared. He was an open-faced, somewhat ruggedly handsome ruddy-haired man who sported a sparse beard and a moustache. Self-assured and well dressed, he was unerringly gracious. As promised, he and Sarah Davis brought out the Flato heart brooch, encrusted with tightly set rubies. Millicent Rogers had helped to design it and I had seen a photo of her wearing it with a tweed suit in 1937. Now it was presented to me in a small rectangular display tray. Sarah and Lee urged me to pin it on. It was strangely inappropriate on my own heather tweed jacket, but I was learning not to turn down chances to share a moment with great jewelry. I posed awkwardly while Sarah snapped a photo with my cell phone.

Soon we got down to business. Lee wondered if I could help him get in touch with the Rogers family. He said he was curious to know if there was more jewelry from Millicent's stellar collection for sale now, sixty-odd years after her death.

He was quick to mention the quid pro quo. If I could help him out a little, perhaps put him in touch with some people, he could probably be of help to me. I didn't know of any way I could use his help at that time, but I admired his candor and energy. Lee is an operator. I liked him for not beating around the bush. I would learn later, from others in his business, that he is considered to be a total natural, a third-generation figure in the jewelry trade. He has an outgoing personality, is well liked by his colleagues and even by his competitors. His father worked in New York's diamond district for years, and Lee is a refinement on the hustling world of the diamond exchange; I would often hear from jewelers in the months ahead, "If I had the money and taste Lee Siegelson does," or, "Lee Siegelson would . . ." Now, he wanted to know where Millicent Rogers's jewelry had gone after her death and if I could put him in touch with the family.

I could not help him. I had to admit, I just hadn't focused that directly on Millicent's jewelry. She had an extensive collection of Native American silver, and she had made jewelry herself out of eighteen-karat gold that she often gave to her friends and lovers. But none of that was what Lee and other New York jewelers were interested in. He mentioned a rumor about a secret safe. I was clueless, and skeptical.

Lee would tell me later of a story he was trying to make sense of. He had heard that a former boyfriend of one of Millicent Rogers's granddaughters had managed to acquire Rogers's ruby and amethyst starfish and some other pieces for several hundred thousand dollars. "Something like that," he said, typically vague when it came to the cost of pieces, but he continued with the story. The fellow had turned around and sold the starfish for at least twice what he had paid for it. Lee had heard of the starfish before, he said. He had taken note when another one, possibly two, had passed through the hands of his friends at Stephen Russell, fine jewelers on Madison Avenue, in previous years. I quickly registered that comment: possibly two? So there was more than one of these exotic pieces? Lee had even been in on one of those deals, I would learn later, although he didn't mention that. I assumed he knew Millicent's starfish had been at Verdura the night of the book party.

He was distressed, he said, that the Rogers piece was heftily marked up when it was shopped around to New York jewelry dealers. Lee would have rather bought directly from the family for a better price and cut out the middleman. I promised when I got home to New Mexico, where I lived, to ask Millicent's granddaughter, who had been a reliable source for me, when I was writing her grandmother's biography, if she would be willing to speak with him.

There was a lot to mull over when I left Siegelson that day, moving into the crowd of shoppers outside of Saks Fifth Avenue, moseying along looking in the windows like any tourist. Normally I didn't stop to ogle the displays in the windows of Cartier and Tiffany, but now as I headed up toward Central Park I stopped to look. The diamond and sapphire pieces on display were nothing like the starfish I had seen. They seemed small, commonplace, compared with the red and purple starfish that I held in my mind. Though large, it had not been loud or gaudy but it had radiated an unmistakable presence. I was thinking about it a lot. And now, I found, there was more than one! And not only was I impressed by the one I had seen, but it was important enough in the jewelry trade for a person of Siegelson's stature to be pursuing it. I also understood that I had just stepped behind the curtain for a peek into a world I had not previously known existed. It wasn't difficult to connect the dots and conclude that the starfish I had seen at Verdura was the same one Lee was talking about that had been bought from the Rogers family. Lee surely knew that but he hadn't come right out and said so. In fact, the whole topic had been treated almost like small talk. Ward hadn't mentioned any backstory when he showed me the brooch at the party. The granddaughter Lee mentioned didn't sound like the one I knew, a new divorcée unlikely to have boyfriends who might try to con her out of her grandmother's fine jewelry. I was starting to see that the jewelry business was a world of some intrigue.

I tried to recall what I knew about the starfish. I had thought that it was just another piece of showy jewelry, de rigueur for an heiress like Rogers, who always sought fine and unique adornments.

She had been casual about jewelry. There had been a diamond necklace she had cavalierly flung upward that clung to a chandelier until her maid found it while cleaning. There were hundreds of pieces of silver and turquoise jewelry in her collections and she had made gold rings and necklaces that their detractors had considered crude designs. I was certain now that I had seen only a black-and-white photo of the starfish before I saw the real thing at Verdura. I also remembered that Rogers, who did have talent for designing jewelry, had been inspired by the jewelry house of Boivin in Paris, where the starfish was made. Boivin was run by women designers known for their animal-like and "barbaric" motifs. That story I remembered. Now it was time to Google. A description of the starfish in Christie's auction listings declared that *three* ruby and amethyst starfish brooches had been made by Boivin and that the American movie actress Claudette Colbert had owned the first one.

When I got home to Taos, New Mexico, where my husband and I had spent most of our time since leaving New York ten years earlier, I dug out my copy of the black-and-white photograph of Rogers from *Vogue* magazine in 1945. She was wearing the starfish with a black Schiaparelli pantsuit. She posed in her New York apartment with one of her beloved dachsunds perched on her desk, the starfish brooch pinned to her right shoulder. The photo, I realized, didn't do it justice. In fact, the first time I had seen the photo, I had taken closer note of the dachsund on the desktop than the jewelry. I clearly wasn't enough of a jewelry fancier for it to catch my eye in black and white. The starfish needed to be seen in color to be captivating.

Several weeks later I received an e-mail from a woman I didn't know. Claudine Seroussi in London. She explained that she researched the history of jewels and was currently writing a booklet for a dealer in London, Lucas Rarities. Her job was putting together a catalogue for a showcase of jewels that included three pieces of Rogers's jewelry. She added that "they were purchased directly from one of her descendants." She attached dazzling color photos of two of them, an emerald and sapphire starburst brooch made by Verdura and an odd hippocamp brooch with a dangling dark pearl that was made by Boivin in Paris.

The third, she explained, was a ruby and amethyst starfish brooch! She was looking for photos of Rogers wearing the starfish beyond the one we both knew of with the dachshund at her desk in New York taken by the photographer Richard Rutledge in 1945. I said I would try to help. I needed to review the photos that I had seen of Millicent. I also needed to think. While I dutifully sorted through the images I had of Rogers I kept running over what Claudine had told me. So the starfish I saw at Verdura's in New York was now at Lucas Rarities in London. In my next exchange I asked Claudine if she knew that the Rogers starfish had been at my book party. She did. It had been sent to Verdura from Lucas Rarities, her employer. "Ward requested it for your party and several days later it was returned to London," she responded, answering the question I had asked Ward but that he had sidestepped.

The query from Seroussi about the starfish picked up my pulse again. I had no idea the starfish was of such interest or so important to jewelers. My excitement was partly due to Seroussi, who was a witty and literate correspondent with the answer to just about anything I asked her. She knew the jewelry business, and she reveled in being able to explain its machinations and identify the players. She was irreverent and funny. Yet I would eventually come to find in Claudine the same anxiety that I learned was endemic to the profession. She worried needlessly, I thought (and hoped), about exposure for talking about a business whose distinguishing feature is secrecy. Sometimes the questions I asked didn't seem very sensitive or controversial to me, but in her world, she told me, they were grenades.

The jewelry trade, I was learning, is a shadow business. Seroussi, who had worked for jewelers in Europe for the past ten years, put it succinctly, explaining to me her own reluctance to be associated with anything that might be written about three pieces of jewelry created nearly eighty years ago. I thought that if I decided to write about the starfish it would be a simple story of a list of owners and dealers who had in one way or another dealt with them. She set me straight. "The jewelry trade is not like the art market. People don't write about players and they don't talk about them. [It is] very private and discreet and in many respects operates in the shadows. This trade runs on reputation. It's as simple as that. The jewelry trade is a very fragile ecosystem within which everything is held by a very delicate balance." She was warning me that even a modest reporting effort was going to meet with resistance.

Shortly after the message from Claudine Seroussi I got up from my desk at home and walked into the living room, where a fire was murmuring in the fireplace. Three ruby and amethyst starfish brooches cartwheeled through my thoughts, sparkling and teasing. They seemed to wink from the real flames. They beckoned me. They were worth chasing.

A different kind of story was unfolding in front of me. I was hearing some tantalizing rumors: Claudette Colbert lost her starfish, or it was stolen, and nobody seemed to know when or where it happened. A legendary Parisienne beauty, a possible starfish owner, persuaded her husband to buy her the jewelry she wanted and to support her lover as well. A Bronx salesman of Mexican crafts and clothing who operated under a prestigious-sounding British name became the industry's top purveyor of classic antique jewelry *and* imitations. I was also starting to hear that there were possibly more than three starfish, maybe even five. I would start with what little I knew about jewelry, do my research, and then tackle the dealers and the experts, the people who knew all about these starfish. If they really knew. And if they would tell me.

Chapter Four

NEEDED TO KNOW MORE ABOUT THE STARFISH AND THE world that had produced them. They obviously had a quality that had survived the fluctuations of taste and value over time while other jewelry slipped into oblivion. When I spoke by phone with British jewelry expert Vivienne Becker, who listed the Boivin ruby and amethyst starfish as one of the one hundred most valuable pieces in the world in her book, *The Impossible Collection of Jewelry*, she explained to me what she considered the starfish's enduring appeal. "It was a superb piece of design timed so well. It was so avant-garde at the time, the size, the mix of colors. The material was used brilliantly to reflect nature in a very unsentimental way. There was the audacity of making something so big and colorful. It was an expression of femininity at the time, strong and bold." She added that the value, and perhaps the design, were influenced by "who owned and who wore them," in much the same way that celebrities boost the value of styles and design today. "Really good jewelry designers are so rare and so exceptional and a good piece of design made in precious materials is even more rare." She had first seen an actual starfish in 2012 in New York when Lee Siegelson had Millicent Rogers's in his salon.

Because I had not handled the starfish at Verdura I had not yet experienced the marvel of its articulated rays, a mechanism so finely tuned that the rays did not dangle loosely when pinned on but caused them to gently conform to the body of the wearer. The articulation made them versatile. There were many curves and contours where they could be pinned and molded to a woman's figure.

The starfish brooches are outsized, but their gems and price tags are not, which can be confusing to novice collectors who consider stones as the best measure of value. Counting carats misses the point. Vintage jewelry as exceptional as the starfish is about equal parts craft and style and history and romance, not gemstone size. Even though the latest sale of a Boivin starfish fell not far beneath a million dollars, many diamonds will exceed that any day. A Boivin ruby and amethyst starfish appeals to a different side of a collector's fancy than does a big rock. Rather than mineral value and financial worth, it is a piece of art, and art typically has a story attached that helps a sophisticated collector appreciate it.

The starfishs' value was rooted in their history. Jewelry design, like both fine and decorative arts once you get beyond the first scratches on the walls by cave dwellers, always owes something to the design ethos that came before. The period of fine jewelry making in the 1930s that had spawned the starfish was a golden—and bygone—era. Its finest attributes were represented in the starfish.

That's one reason they are counted among the most spectacular pieces of the twentieth century.[1]

I stopped for a bemused moment to consider my own qualifications as a chronicler of such exotic and sumptuous pieces. Beyond being a reporter and a writer I had none. Except, I noted whimsically, the brooches had a lot of rubies, and ruby was my birthstone. So why not, I reasoned, start my research there?

I was given a ruby about the size of a grain of cracked wheat, set in a gold ring, by my grandmother when I was seven. My parents replaced it later with another, a slightly larger oval stone set in a little gold mesh screen. It was purchased at the town jewelry store on Main Street around the corner from our house in Richmond, Indiana.

That store, like so many small-town institutions that dotted main streets before merchants moved to malls, sold mostly engagement rings, charms for charm bracelets, lavalieres, and high school rings. Its big storefront window and interior glass jewelry cases made it a favorite place for me and my junior high girlfriends to burn time when we walked home after school. The clerks were endlessly patient as we asked to see this charm and that, to try on rings we had no chance of buying, and to look at post earrings, although we didn't have pierced ears. That was about the extent of one's jewelry needs in Richmond, until you graduated from high school or became engaged, and I did neither there. My grandmother, an antiques dealer, gave me another ring with two small rubies cupped in open gold roses. It snagged on sweaters and towels. I left it on the edge of the bathtub in the Jefferson Hotel in Washington, D.C., many years later and never saw it again.

I never bothered to think about the quality of stones or where they came from until I encountered the Boivin starfish. But now I was making the connection between that storefront in Indiana and the glorious pieces that had captivated me. Design is the crowning glory of the brooches, but their attraction for me had started with the stones.

The raw elements of these pieces, even before the storied French creators and the glamorous owners, have their own illustrious history. Rubies were first mentioned in recorded history in literature about the Northern Silk Road of China in 200 B.C. Always valued highly in Asian countries, they were used to ornament armor, scabbards, and harnesses of Indian and Chinese noblemen. Cleopatra draped herself in both precious and semiprecious jewels, rubies among them, when she reclined under her gold-spangled canopy. They came into more popular usage and fashion in Europe at the turn of the twentieth century. Some thirty years later, Boivin's starfish were spawned on a drawing desk in Paris.

I did some homework.

The most desirable ruby stones are bloodred, or "pigeon's blood." Legend has it that they were named by the Chinese, who prized them for matching the shade of a drop of pigeon's blood on a silver tray. For eight hundred years the best have been mined in Burma (Upper Myanmar), in the Mogok Valley, a region four hundred miles north of Rangoon. They have been mined in Thailand, Cambodia, India, Afghanistan, and even more recently in Kenya and Montana in the United States, but the finest have most often come from Burma, as did the stones in Boivin's ruby starfish.

The seventy-one rubies that went into each of Boivin's ruby and amethyst starfish were cabochons, stones shaped and polished to a rounded dome with a flat bottom, rather than faceted. They were prized for their intense color and often used in crowns of kings and noblemen. But normally, Boivin made a point of not buying the finest gemstones because the value of its jewelry, in the minds of the Boivins and their designers, was derived from workmanship and design rather than the worth of gems. The balance between the value of the stones and the less tangible aesthetic appeal was invariably tipped toward the latter. It's a bit like the execution of a good French pastry that owes more to its baker than the raw, albeit high-quality, ingredients used to make it.

Amethysts, on the other hand, are semiprecious stones, a quartz crystal in fact. It was bold of Boivin to pair them, purely for their purplish color, with precious red rubies. Before the nineteenth century amethysts had been nearly as expensive as precious stones and appeared in the crowns and jewelry of royals, but a large deposit discovered in Brazil in 1902 lowered their price and flooded the gem market. They have been a favorite of mass market jewelers ever since. The name amethyst, which means "not drunk" in ancient Greek, has caused some wearers to believe the stones protect against drunkenness. Others claim they stave off seduction, and I suspect there's rightly a connection to drinking there. A whole list of metaphysical properties has been assigned to amethysts, including the inducement of peace and calm, reduction of compulsive behavior, reduction of grief, and healing. I was reminded of a huge pinkish purple quartz that decorates the entry of a hotel in Taos that aims to conjure up a metaphysical and mystical atmosphere, considered "woo-woo" by skeptical locals.

The mix of precious and semiprecious stones can puzzle the inexperienced jewelry connoisseur. Starfish are not Hope diamonds. They do not command the price of large showpiece gems. Gemstones, "rocks" in some jewelers' parlance, come and go, but the design and workmanship of a jewelry master from the early nineteenth century cannot be replicated. So while the starfish are not as highly valued as a large raw diamond they are certainly worth more than the sum of the values of their rubies and amethysts and their eighteen-karat-gold setting. It is the alchemy between design and gems that determines the worth.

The dash of daring in the creation of the starfish displayed by pairing rubies with amethysts was part of the Boivin appeal and one reason French jewelry historian Françoise Cailles, who authenticates Boivin jewelry for dealers, noted, "I have frequently noticed that collectors develop a surprisingly strong attachment to Boivin jewels. Very few pieces, in fact, ever come on the market because no matter when they were made, their resolutely modern concept permits them to adapt perfectly to the lifestyle and dress of today." This observation by Cailles, which has the sturdy ring of a sales pitch, is nevertheless an apt description of Boivin jewelry's appeal. It was eerily echoed in many conversations I have had with the sellers and dealers of Boivin's starfish.

"Emeralds go up and down with the market. Diamonds go up and down, but beautiful pieces never go out of style. If you look at anything that has a name and is beautifully made it never goes out of fashion," explained Daphne Lingon, a senior vice president and jewelry specialist at Christie's in New York. The starfish, in her opinion, are immune from fluctuations in value and changes in fashion. "People will always want them," she said.

Cailles told me that Jeanne Boivin did not need to travel to Burma or other ports where the stones used in her pieces were found. In the booming jewelry business of the 1930s, everything came to Paris. Boivin had a lapidary in the workroom behind her salon who helped acquire, cut, polish, and set gemstones. A picture of the bustling world of gem sales and dealers was given me by another jeweler and focused on a pearl merchant in London as late as the 1970s. In a scene that sounds more like the current stock exchange, stones would be auctioned at gem markets. Jewelers remember that one man, Abe Cohen, had a corner on the pearl market and so sharp was his eye and astute his valuations that when the representatives of major jewelry stores watched from the balcony to see what he bid on, they hurried to follow suit and price their acquisitions accordingly. Cohen's ability to judge a pearl or stone was considered prescient, uncanny even. And after a while, his judgment was self-fulfilling. What he pronounced became fact. He was feared. As I moved through the jewelry community I noted that even in modern times and northern climates, when merchants and sellers wear suits and wingtip shoes into the marketplace, the customs and expressions of gem merchants are barely removed from the culture of the souk, where stone trading first began.

Of course, with jewelry, perception is as important as any science, perhaps more so. One does not buy a diamond ring because it is hard enough to score a plate-glass window. One buys a diamond ring because it symbolizes commitment and lasting love. It was De Beers, the world's largest diamond merchant, that proclaimed that connection with its creation of the legendary slogan "A diamond is forever." Who is to say it isn't so? Similarly, rubies come to mean more than a July birthday. Passion, desire, opulence, and power are all suggested by small red stones the size of a pomegranate seed. With people, it is what is conjured in the mind and senses that counts.

If I had ever doubted it, a scene from a fine arts fair in New York's Armory on Park Avenue made me a believer. I watched a man whom I supposed to be a dealer take a gold Boivin ring from its case and give it a sniff. I asked him what he was doing. "You can smell who owned it," he explained haughtily as he threw a glance at me as though I'd asked about his sex life. I didn't ask him who it smelled like. It was probably unromantic of me to think it would most likely carry the scent of hand cream from whoever had tried it on before him. But this was not the last time I would be told that jewelry carries history in its scent.

Chapter Five

N THE EARLY 1900S, PARIS WAS THE CULTURAL CAPITAL OF the world. It set fashions in dress, art, and pleasure for no greater reason than that there was suddenly a wealthy class of people who paid no taxes and didn't really work. Their world was one of great excesses, frivolity, cultivated taste, luxury, and relaxed morals. The city had emerged from the Franco-Prussian War with a great burst of construction and beautiful architecture. Other European cities at the time, notes historian and writer Roger Shattuck, were former villages that expanded out beyond a few grand palaces at the center. Paris was a great world stage for theater, both at the real Opéra and on the street, in the salons of its citizens and the public cafés. Fashion influenced every quarter of life in a world that went out to see and be seen from almost noon until midnight.

Boivin's timing for entering the jewelry business was fortuitous. The appetite for fine jewelry was growing rapidly. In the early twentieth century in Paris, a man's economic ascent was often measured by the jewels that his wife wore.[1] Some women became famous simply because of their jewels, whether they were countesses, courtesans, or merely society beauties. Empress Josephine had an endless craving for jewels and finery. Queen Alexandra of England and the Grand Duchess Wladimir of Russia, known for their ostentation, appeared totally encrusted when they stepped out in public. Countess Greffulhe of France became a symbol of international elegance by spending huge sums on her jewelry and wardrobe at a time when fortunes were not yet eroded by taxation.

It was the French, of course, who made jewelry design into an art rather than a craft, as it had begun. The Belle Epoque, between 1890 and 1914, drew to a close with the start of World War I, but its influence on design stretched far into the twentieth century. The creative arts in Paris were then, postwar, fueled by new European and American millionaires. From the time of Napoleon III, France had consistently pursued a policy of supporting and promoting luxury goods, designed to extend France's influence and promote Paris as the European capital of good taste. Russian grand dukes considered Paris to be their second capital of luxury and joined in the pleasures.

During the Belle Epoque, in which the avant-garde became prominent in France, fashion influenced every domain of life. The traditions and reserve of the nineteenth century were left behind in a kind of swagger that affected style, literature, morals, and society. The Eiffel Tower was built in this era, fashion magazines were first published, scientists, painters, and writers all tilted toward the future. Salons and banquets symbolized the moment. Impressionism spread throughout the art world. Ravel, Debussy, and Satie revolutionized contemporary music. D. H. Lawrence and

James Joyce were making their reputations for modernizing literature while living and writing in Paris. Shattuck called it "a lusty banquet of the arts."

The new moneyed class's appetite for quality and decorative novelty converged to make designers of all kinds of adornment, if not exactly rich, at least prosperous. Wealthy Americans, especially those with the newly minted riches of the robber barons with their oilfields and railroad fortunes, had by the twenties joined the craze for extravagant and beautiful things. Jewelry was no longer, as it had been for Catherine the Great, a perk of royalty. She had used her stash to reward friends for loyalty and to finance armies. These newer rich were accumulating their own fine jewelry. Small creations to adorn a bodice or dangle from an earlobe were the intimate embodiment of the trend. They were riches you could hold in your hand, show off, and keep close.

It was just as the city was blossoming that René Boivin became a jewelry designer. Born into a modest family of goldsmiths in 1864, he wanted to become a doctor, but his family's financial struggles required him to enter the family business as soon as he graduated from high school at seventeen and work as a goldsmith with his elder brother. He took drawing lessons and showed a talent for making jewelry, especially engraving, and then he learned the respected craft of jewelry making by training with Parisian craftsmen in the world of decorative arts. Determinedly, he attended various workshops to learn the trade, and by the time he was twenty-five he was recognized as a master, known for his draftsmanship. It was a good time to achieve that designation, since the era of the master jeweler had just begun, and those who earned the title, like Fabergé and Lalique, were elevated to a class above once anonymous tradesmen. Their professional and social status was closer to that of an artist, perhaps more like that of celebrated architects today, who have the genius to present a concept that others will produce to specification.

René Boivin increased his chances for success when he married Jeanne Poiret, the sister of the rising dress designer Paul Poiret. The two made a potent combination. As designers they rubbed shoulders with the intellectuals and trendsetters of their day. The Boivin jewelry salon functioned as a gathering place for Erik Satie, Sigmund Freud, and other well-known personages in Paris who befriended its owners, René and Jeanne. It became a salon of sorts, where people appeared as much for the elevated company as the jewelry. But Boivin was establishing a tradition as well of true craft and design genius.[2]

For those of us who see jewelry only when it is for sale in a well-lit display case or while watching a jeweler hunched over his table making repairs to a watch or bracelet clasp, its origin is a mystery. The intricacies of making fine jewelry are both a surprisingly exotic art and a flat-footed trade at once. It was even more so in Paris in the late 1800s when Boivin began. A jeweler, understanding the properties of the metals and stones available to him, would draw a design, then the actual making of the piece would be turned over to a workshop that specialized in fine metalwork. Many jewelers had their own workshop on the premises, but if it could not keep up with demand, or the design required specialized skills beyond those available in-house, the work was farmed out to others. Some workshops excelled at engraving, others at stone setting, yet others at the mechanics of movable parts. It was important for a good jeweler to have relationships with the workshops whose skills could help realize his designs. Unlike today, when lasers and technology make it possible to industrialize and mass-produce jewelry, in the early twentieth century it was an art that was practiced by skilled artisans, the "golden hands" who labored to make every piece as perfect as possible. Most were paid by the piece, not by the hour. Keeping man-hours to a minimum was not a critical part of the process, which is perhaps a reason that the jewelry from this period rose to such high standards of quality. The designer and fabricator in the workshop were partners in the pursuit of perfection in gold and gemstones rather than high efficiency for a mass market. It was not unusual for a design to pass through another half-dozen hands of specialists at each stage of production before a finished piece of jewelry emerged in the showroom.

René Boivin and his wife started modestly, as did most jewelry craftsmen at the time. They lived in an apartment facing their workshop at 38 Rue de Turbigo. While Boivin designed, Jeanne kept the books and oversaw the accounts. Boivin was making a reputation for his engraving; the Paris department store Le Bon Marché and jewelers like Clerc and Boucheron carried his designs. A bestiary of imaginative and sometimes mythological creatures, especially cats, was popular. Griffons, peacocks, and chimeras turned up in his designs. Though he designed clocks, vases, and candelabra, it was a turn toward graceful naturalism that distinguished his work. An avid gardener, he loved flowers and subscribed to botany magazines for inspiration. His brooches of flower sprays and blossoms caught on with a public that wanted floral naturalism in jeweled necklaces and a variety of pins for bodices and dresses. He excelled at creating delicate blossoms out of gold and diamonds, usually daisies or wild roses, but his range included thistles, irises, lilies, and even orchids. His flowers were encrusted with diamonds. Their delicate mountings enabled them to tremble with any movement, a trait the French called *en trem-blant*. It was a trend in the pieces created at Boivin that would mature over the years and point toward the starfish to come.[3]

Art Nouveau had taken Paris by storm in 1900 after the World's Fair, visited by 30 million people. The star of this design world was René Lalique, a designer in glass and jewelry whose contributions to Art Nouveau thrust jewelry into the public consciousness as a major art form. The public was hungry for novelty to accompany its symbols of wealth and prestige. Yet while the importance of jewelry in French fashion soared, René Boivin was not swept away by Art Nouveau trends. If he gave a nod to the Nouveau style it was that he incorporated more flat jewelry and fewer of the *tremblant*-type projections onto his pieces as time went on. The designs were simpler, the settings heavier. Design seemed to triumph over delicacy. When he began working with semiprecious stones, he moved in the direction that would distinguish Boivin jewelry later, up into the thirties and forties. Topazes, tourmalines, amethysts, even moonstones began turning up in jewelry designs that had emphasized diamonds a decade earlier. He used wood inlaid with pearls, and his creation of large raised signet rings, a natural for an engraver, sparked a lasting trend in women's rings. Never content to stand still, he expanded into exotica and designed jewelry with a Persian flavor. He created pendants with pavé-set stones on platinum or black-enameled gold. Connoisseurs of quality and luxury goods were his clients. The House of Boivin boasted clients from the Middle East and South America as well as the commissions of a sophisticated and demanding clientele in Paris that was willing to pay high prices. Persistent and energetic in his pursuit of beautiful objects, Boivin also collected antiques and exhibition pieces. He was partial to boxes, flasks, cases, aigrettes, all things with special appeal to an engraver.

The Boivin salon now occupied space at the tonier Rue des Pyramides address. René and Jeanne, who had three children, moved into a wonderful and spacious apartment on the Boulevard Haussman in 1907. The next decade was a prosperous and influential period for his wife Jeanne and her brother, Paul, by then Paris's leading couturier. Children of a textile merchant, Paul Poiret and his sister, Jeanne Boivin, had risen to the top levels of

Parisian design and fashion society. Poiret designed clothes to satisfy a trend that had taken Paris by storm after the opening of Diaghilev's Ballets Russes production of *Sheherazade* in 1910. He quickly ascended into the Paris fashion elite and became the most sought-after couturier of his time with collections of bold and theatrical styles.[4] Opulent costumes in hues of emerald green, vermilion, orange, and carmine worn to depict life in a sultan's harem electrified the public and sparked the advent of a vivid Orientalism in fashion circles.[5] The well-publicized archaeological discovery of royal tombs and their cache of treasures by two British explorers in Thebes, Egypt, added a shot of pharaonic inspiration to the appetite for new exotic styles. Poiret added Turkish trousers and loose-flowing styles to his creations, occasionally topping a turban with an aigrette or other piece of jewelry. A jewelry clientele that had somewhat conservatively preferred diamonds suddenly fell in love with lush stones and colors. Boivin began designing bold, colorful jewelry for Poiret's collections and soon fashion icons such as Elsa Schiaparelli and Diana Vreeland, as well as artists and intellectuals, trooped to the Boivin salon. Poiret declared that he would rather stage lavish parties than spend money on advertising, and the ploy worked admirably well for Jeanne and René, who partied hard along with him as photographs of the pair in an array of elaborate costumes, almost comic by standards today, illustrate. The alchemy of fun and fashion was powerful and attracted artists and intelligentsia to the spirit of their jewelry.[6]

Poiret often brought his celebrity clientele to his sister's apartment where, if they had not already discovered the gracious Boivins and René's work, they were introduced to the perfect accessories for their dresses and gowns. Their imposing size, bold proportions, and brightly colored jewels were perfect for Poiret's creations. It was an ideal convergence of fraternal marketing. So gracious and fashionable were the Boivin salons that clients and friends dropped by to simply hang out. Not only did the Boivins have the salon, that fashionable room where jewelry was designed and sold, but they also presided over their *salon*, that uniquely French social tradition of hosting an assemblage of notable and fashionable persons for conversation and conviviality. The salon was no longer open to "passing trade" but by appointment only. Life was good. But it was about to change.

Boivin went to war to defend France in World War I and, like more than a million other Frenchmen to die in service to their country, he never returned. Ironically, rather than ending the story of Boivin, his death set the stage for a second chapter that would distinguish the House of Boivin perhaps even more than his design legacy.

Jeanne Boivin lost both her husband and their son Pierre in the war. The public expected her to shutter and close the business, but she had been running the accounting and operations side of the jewelry house for her husband for years, and she had relationships with the workshops and craftsmen that accounted for the high quality of Boivin pieces, so she quietly continued fulfilling orders and became the first woman in Paris to run a major jewelry house. Jewelry in the 1920s was considered a man's business and there was prejudice against her, but demand continued for the consistently beautiful and well-designed pieces Boivin produced. So long as she kept up the standards of the work, no one truly cared what gender she was. She would in time leave her own distinctive mark on the jewelry business.

The war brought an end to the new relaxed frivolity in fashion and jewelry. Precious metals became scarce, especially platinum, which was essential in the armament industry. The British government outlawed trading it. And as fashion often does in wartime, the jewelry business contracted. Fine pieces were sold or stashed away for security, like savings. The leading French jeweler Cartier produced diamond brooches and pendants using the symbols of war such as cannons and fighter airplanes to capture the spirit of the public. Not much feminine fun and expression there. It would be the 1920s before style was reinvigorated.

Jewelry was reintroduced into women's fashion with a vengeance in the 1920s. Even scantily clad flappers and free spirits loved to cover themselves in glittering jewels and bling. *Sautoirs,* long necklaces with tassels or ornaments at the ends, were gayly tossed down the bare backs of daringly low-cut dresses. Fashion-conscious women wore multiple bracelets on bare arms and bandeaux, sometimes punctuated with a brooch, across their foreheads at night. "Jewels became an accessory, strictly dependent on the shape and color of the dress on which they were worn, rather than a precious ornament to represent a display of wealth as had been the case in the prewar years," explained David Bennett and Daniela Mascetti in their book *Understanding Jewellery.* Floral-spray brooches of the nineteenth century, even corsage ornaments, weren't suited to the loosely fitted, freely moving fashions of the twenties. Some women, striving for perfection, went so far as to have clothes designed to match a piece of jewelry. Clothing and jewelry were even more inextricably bound together, and new creative freedom began to creep back into style.

The brooch itself had evolved through history, from the Bronze Age, and was born of functional need. Broochlike pins and fasteners held primitive garments closed. In the eighteenth century they were adopted by men to adorn their hats, just that little extra personalized splash that distinguished a man's style, like the small feathers that were tucked into hatbands in the 1950s. Women adopted brooches called *devant-de-corsages* in the early 1900s. They were sewn directly into the dresses, which typically featured a fitted bodice and therefore did not need a pin to secure them. They were permanent fixtures. When bodices went out of fashion, so did corsage ornaments, leaving a vacuum that came to be filled by the brooch. It could be a focal point of a solid-color dress, a feminine touch on a tailored suit, even a little fillip on a handbag or in one's hair. It could be worn imaginatively on various dresses. It was versatile—and showy.

Jeanne Boivin's relationships with the workshops where her jewelry was actually manufactured greatly contributed to her rising eminence. She dutifully maintained those relationships after the death of her husband. At the height of Boivin's popularity and success in the thirties and forties, when orders from Boivin kept a half-dozen workshops busy for months at a time, she had her own workmaster and lapidary in the workroom behind her salon, but she often outsourced work to specialists. With confidence, she and her designers strained the bounds of imagination to make jewelry that had not been seen before.

In the 1930s and 1940s, when Paris and the jewelry business were booming, the "statement brooch" became fashionable, especially since it could be pinned to the structured bodices of the new classic tailored suits and fitted dresses. Flowers perished, but a diamond orchid or lily stayed fresh. Ironically, the stock market crash of 1929 did not make women more restrained about their jewelry, the way hard times are often accompanied by relaxed hemlines. To the contrary, those women with money to buy jewelry opted for bigger, chunkier bracelets and designs, almost like power jewelry today. The trend reflected a phenomenon in entertainment, especially the movies, during lean times. The public, and fashion, preferred symbols of wealth and luxury as a kind of escapism. It was evidence that buying and wearing jewelry was—and is—an outward expression of fantasy.

The time was ripe for Claudette Colbert when she arrived at Boivin, eager for something different. One can imagine her, a movie star known for her impeccable makeup, turned out in one of her favorite classic Travis Banton suits, sitting across from Madame Boivin and Juliette Moutard as they discussed the starfish, much the way stylists do for runway models today. Juliette and Madame didn't fawn over people, but they conspired to make bold creations that would appeal to their bold clientele. The relationship between a woman and her jeweler, who made custom designs to adorn the face and figure seated before her, was a highly luxurious and intimate involvement that created a rarefied bond between the two. It was not merely a financial transaction. The attention-getting Boivin starfish, with its cutting-edge design and miraculously hinged joints that allowed it to conform to the profile of the wearer, was more personalized and intimate yet. This was not just a pin to be stuck onto a collar or neckline. It almost grasped (not groped) its wearer. A woman didn't pin on a Boivin ruby and amethyst starfish without making a commitment to wearing it.

Chapter Six

EXPECTED THAT IMMERSING MYSELF IN THE WORLD OF jewelry dealers, the people who are driven by the financial side of the business, would dispel any romantic expectations I had about jewelry, but I discovered exactly the opposite. The people who worked in the jewelry trade were the most romantic people I had ever met. Sure, money drove many of them, but if you can believe what they tell you, they love their work. I remembered Ward Landrigan telling me how the jewelry business seduced him as a boy in his hometown of Springfield, New Jersey. In order to earn his badge and sash in the Boy Scouts he was required to get a Social Security card and working papers. He was hired by a local jeweler to work in the store after school and holidays. What intrigued him was watching women shoppers put on jewelry and look at themselves in the mirror. "They would purse their lips."

He still remembers how magical it seemed to him. "I was awestruck by jewelry," he confided. The effect that jewelry had on people was what drew him into the business. "That and that you can hold it in your hand and it's beautiful," he added. Every jeweler I met but one spoke of jewelry's tangible gratification. The pieces, the glittering prizes, seemed to soothe and hypnotize them.

It was a rainy summer day when I stopped by the Stephen Russell jewelry salon on Madison Avenue and Sixty-fourth Street in New York. I was on the Upper East Side on other business when I looked across the street and noticed the store that I had planned to visit later. I decided to stop in and get out of the rain. I must have walked past the awninged salon on the corner dozens of times when I lived in New York, but I never took real notice of it. When Lee Siegelson mentioned to me that Stephen Russell had been his partner in owning one of the starfish, I assumed Stephen Russell was one man, but the name is an amalgam of Stephen Feuerman and Russell Zelenetz, business partners. Lee had also told me that at least one of the three Boivin starfish had passed through Stephen Russell in recent years.

Even the small storefront entrance had two glass doors to get inside. A doorman built like a prize fighter whose biceps and back muscles bulged through his well-tailored suit let me in after I buzzed. When I asked if the owners were available he hit a buzzer and wordlessly summoned a salesperson from down in the basement, where the business offices are located. I took a seat in front of a little French provincial desk at the back of the salon in a small alcove. A deep blue and gold brocade curtain was draped to one side and held by a gold tassel behind the desk. I looked around the Art Deco–inspired interior as I waited. Russell Zelenetz, dark-haired and smooth-shaven, burst up the stairs in a crisply ironed purple-striped shirt. His eyes were brown and warm as coffee beans. His smile was wide. I watched his expansiveness contract almost perceptibly and his guard rise when I explained that I was not a shopper, but a writer, looking for information about the Boivin starfish. When I mentioned Lee Siegelson, he softened a little. There was no one in the salon except the two of us and I figured maybe he would talk with me just to bide time until the rain stopped and more people would be on the street. Sure, he said, he had time to talk. And yes, he added somewhat proudly, he had seen *three* ruby and amethyst starfish. Eureka, I thought. I had come in just to test the waters and was surprised to learn that this little jewel box of a jewelry house would have had such exposure to the starfish. My astonishment must have shown because Russell explained to me that Stephen Russell, in contrast to Verdura, which is a gallery retailer, and Siegelson, who is a trader, manages collections and sells from its storefront to the public. These distinctions matter in the jewelry business. It should have come as no surprise that Stephen Russell would partner on certain acquisitions and sales with Lee Siegelson. Siegelson, whose pockets were deep, would acquire a piece of jewelry and then move it on to a dealer like Stephen Russell who had relationships with private clients. Still, I was impressed that Stephen Russell had experience with all three starfish.

Then he asked me a question. "Why do you say there were three of them?" I explained that was what I had learned from the histories on auction sheets and it was the prevailing knowledge about the starfish. What did he think? I asked. "More like five," he said. I was startled again. I began to ask lots of questions. It seemed that a few starfish had been made in the 1980s, some even bearing the Boivin name, but they were larger than the original and somewhat easy to identify as later models. I picked my words carefully. Evidence of additional starfish made me uneasy. Just how many were there? Who had made them? There was a pause when I asked him for a count. There might have been a fourth made in Paris in the 1930s, he said, and then, haltingly, he added there had been some made in the 1980s. I had heard this rumor, and further, had heard that Murray Mondschein might have been involved. Mondschein, a cabdriver's son from the Bronx who sold Mexican arts and crafts, had transformed himself into Fred Leighton, one of Madison Avenue's finest names in jewelry, a dominant personality in the field. I took a leap. Was Mondschein involved? I asked. Yes, said Zelenetz lightly, moving on to add that he had seen a "later starfish," but "I didn't like it." He was telling me, in short, that Stephen Russell only trafficked in originals, but he tiptoed delicately around this mention of Murray.

I was concerned that these later starfish would cloud the matter and skew my reporting if they could not be distinguished from the originals. I wondered if the workmanship and design were as wonderful as the one I had seen. The idea that there might be an assembly line in the Bronx, Paris, or anywhere else stamping out copies horrified me. Would they dilute the treasure pool I was exploring? Russell shrugged. Murray, a legend in the New York jewelry business but reportedly now retired, was the uncle of his partner, Feuerman, I would soon learn.

We glanced off the subject, and I was somewhat reassured that while there might be five starfish moving around, the three that were my quarry were the originals. The possibility that there were more posed nagging questions and could make the job of identifying them more difficult. Five starfish in the world still weren't very many, Russell added, reassuringly. They were still rare, and the later ones were distinguishable from the originals, he said. That seemed to get talk of any troublesome reproductions out of the way for the moment.

I could see that the more questions I asked the more frustrated Russell became. We were limited by our roles: I wanted the kind of information that it was part of his job to withhold. We circled our subject. I sensed he often knew the answers to what I was asking but he wasn't telling me, especially about who owned the starfish now. "The worst thing that can happen in this business is to reveal a buyer. Everything is confidential," he explained. He added that it was rare to know the lineage of a single piece of jewelry. Jewelers are more concerned with authenticity. Is a piece of jewelry what the seller says it is, made by the designer the seller claims and containing the stones the seller says it does? Beyond that, dealers don't care a lot about a piece of jewelry's history of ownership, unless it has been held by someone famous, which would increase its perceived value. Of course, the Boivin starfish, and a few other pieces such as the Van Cleef tutti-frutti bracelets, attracted well-known and often glamorous buyers whose names become associated with the designs when they are talked about, but it is rare to know the exact provenance and complete lineage of a single piece through the decades. If I didn't know already, I was beginning to understand how difficult the goal I had set myself was going to be. I would be able to learn where starfish had been and who some of the owners of them had been over time, but I might never be able to draw a straight line and know exactly which starfish had belonged to whom. This was not going to be a straightforward reporting job, I knew already.

I asked Russell to talk to me about what he could. We exchanged awkward conspiratorial smiles. He had first seen a Boivin ruby and amethyst starfish brooch in 2006. He had seen another in 2008, and he had recently seen one that had gone to a private collector. I figured that was the one that had belonged to Millicent Rogers that Lee Siegelson had recently bought or sold, the one he had been chasing when he invited me to his office salon to meet him and was advertising to his clients when I saw him several months later in Palm Beach. But I might have been a step behind.

Russell was far more forthcoming when talking about the joys of being in the jewelry business. "It's a passion," he said brightening. "You can't think of it strictly as a business." Stephen Russell had been in business almost twenty years, having moved to its East Side location from the Trump Tower address downtown in 2008. When a young woman in jeans arrived at the front door our conversation stalled. She was soon joined by an older woman, presumably her mother, and the two of them got down to the serious business of looking at vintage diamond earrings with Russell's partner, Stephen Feuerman. He is an open-faced sandy-haired man with a vague resemblance to Albert Finney. When he was listening he cocked his head in a way that reminded me of a Welsh terrier I once owned. When the shoppers left, both men grew easier. They wanted to talk about themselves and how they got into the jewelry business. Both were students of fine art and design. They spoke emotionally about their feelings for certain fine pieces they've handled. In one instance a necklace was sold, but the buyer postponed collecting it. Eventually he changed his mind and decided not to buy it. "We were so relieved because we liked being near it," Russell admitted. Stephen agreed. Eventually the necklace sold to someone else, someone the two men felt better about having it. If someone had come into our conversation late and not known the subject, he or she might have thought we were talking about a dog rather than a piece of jewelry. Russell and Stephen told me they felt the same way about an Alexander Calder necklace that Stephen said he felt real affection for. "I was happier when it was still here." He shrugged. Their enthusiasm for jewelry extends to their private time, as well. They both said that when they were on vacation they scouted for jewelry. During a recent air travel delay Russell was stranded in Dallas. He called ahead to Stephen to tell him he would be returning late to New York. "What are you going to do with yourself while you're there?" Stephen asked. Russell told him he was heading into the city to look around at jewelry.

I had to ask what it was about the starfish that had attracted them. There were pieces of jewelry worth more money. Designs that were easier to sell. "The first time I saw it I just loved it. Always," said Russell, like a true lover. It was the starfish's beauty that had impressed him and has caused him to pursue them whenever one has been in reach. He was the closest I would come to meeting a starfish hunter, one who went out of his way to track down and buy a starfish. Indeed, as I became able to draw a trail for the starfish, three of them would pass through Stephen Russell. Russell unapologetically explained that devotion such as his is subjective. "Jewelry is almost like art. If you don't like it, it doesn't matter what it's worth," he declared with that jeweler's hubris I would come to love and distrust.

When I left Stephen Russell I knew Murray Mondschein was going to be an important presence in my quest. I can't recall who first mentioned him to me, though I was quick to learn that "Murray" is spoken of like a godfather in the jewelry world. Neither do I remember how I learned that Fred Leighton and Murray Mondschein are synonymous. Everyone assumes that everyone else already knows. Murray is one of the most important jewelers in the world. Now eighty-two, he has been on the jewelry scene since the 1970s. When I asked Ward Landrigan at Verdura when he had first seen or become conscious of the Boivin ruby and amethyst starfish brooches, he paused to think back. "The first time I saw it was at Murray's." That was back in the 1980s when Ward worked at Christie's. "I thought, my God, that's fabulous," Ward remembered. "There was just something about it," he recalled. It was the red and purple color combination, unusual in his opinion, that made a lasting impression.

Chapter Seven

THE STARFISHS' VALUE, I HAD HEARD OVER AND OVER
again, rested not in the value of their gemstones, but in
their design. I wanted to know what had inspired them.
In a sense, I was asking how starfish are born, and I wished
the question had been as easy to answer as learning about starfish
in the ocean.

My quest would draw me back to Jeanne Boivin and the ways
that she had guided her jewelry house in new directions after her
husband's death. She hung on to the master jewelers who kept
Boivin's quality high, but the designs that flourished under her direction were different from the Cubist and geometric styles that
were popularized during the Art Deco rage. These designs were
softer, figurative, and feminine. Like her brother, who had rejected
corsets for women's styles, she chafed against bourgeois "good

taste," which she considered to be stultifying and uninspired.[1] Rather, Jeanne sought styles in jewelry that were figurative and suited to women, their fluid body movements, and their clothes. Much of the jewelry of the time more closely resembled military insignia. Boivin's was informed by a new philosophy that embraced sumptuousness and exotic forms. It was not surprising that wealthy trendsetters like Louise de Vilmorin, who was considered the most stylish woman in Paris in the twenties and thirties, European royalty, American movie stars, and stylish American heiresses had all climbed the stairs to the Boivin atelier. De Vilmorin came with her handbag brimming with francs but always stashed one bank note back into her bag as she left. She explained it would be her reason for returning to visit with her friend Jeanne.[2] Business and society strode side by side in the jewelry business at the time. The world of rich and fashionable clients was relatively small by today's global standards, and word traveled fast about Jeanne Boivin's distinctively chic new designs and the pleasure of basking in the glow of her charming jewelry salon.

Inspiration for design is more difficult to assign. It was assumed that René Boivin incorporated flowers into his jewelry designs because he was an avid gardener—and the flowers showed up in his sketchbooks. Jeanne Boivin took long walks along the coast of Brittany that put her in mind of seashells, pebbles, branches, and other bits of nature along the shore. Whatever sparked it, a fresh naturalist influence began to creep into Boivin designs. Shells and sea creatures were often cast in gold. Madame Boivin asked her designers for seashells, and one young new designer in particular heeded her call.

The progression of the Boivin look and style owes a great deal to a young designer whom Jeanne Boivin hired in 1925. Suzanne Belperron started as a salesgirl but would go on to great design fame, as a recent retrospective of her designs at Christie's in 2012 attests. Jeanne began to teach her the tools of the trade and

Belperron's real talent soon emerged. Though she is often referred to as a former sales clerk because that was her entry-level job
at Boivin, in fact, Belperron had already studied design when she
took the position. She moved quickly out of sales and into the
workshop, where she made her way into the pantheon of great jewelry designers of the twentieth century. The five years that she
spent at Boivin seemed to solidify the house's reputation as a bas-
tion of innovative women designers. The jewelry they made derived
its primary value from original design and excellent craftsmanship
rather than simply the quality and worth of the gemstones. This
would become a distinguishing characteristic of Boivin jewelry and
ultimately a way of knowing its creator, especially since Jeanne
Boivin and Suzanne Belperron did not sign or otherwise mark
their jewelry. They stubbornly believed that the eminent design,
at least its distinctive character, was evidence enough of who had
made the pieces that came out of the salon. It hardly came as a
surprise that when Suzanne Belperron's work began to embody
her own personal style, these two strong-minded women would
conflict. According to a former employee of Boivin, both were
obstinate and strong-willed, and in 1930, Belperron left Boivin.

The concern, as in most jewelry business ruptures, was that
the younger designer would also take clients and designs with
her. The matter of creative ownership plagues jewelers. Jeanne
would continue to think that Belperron's talent was a hybrid of
their collaboration, though Belperron and her followers see her as
an original genius. The different point of view still sparks quarrels
in the jewelry community.

In trying to assign provenance to the Boivin starfish, Suzanne
Belperron is often suggested. There are several starfish in her
sketchbook. They are chubbier and smaller overall than the ruby
and amethyst starfish, and in the drawings, at least, they have little
curls at the ends of all the arms, whereas an identifying feature of
the Boivin starfish is that two rays of each starfish are flipped at

their ends. There seems to be no question that while Belperron was employed at Boivin, her employer, Jeanne, requested seashell and other maritime designs. It is also easy to assume that all fine Boivin design during her tenure and shortly thereafter was inspired by Belperron because her archives are accessible and Olivier Baroin, a French jeweler and archivist who has digitized them, is a champion of her work. As recently as 2012, Cathy Horyn wrote in *The New York Times* that "her designs are so singular—bold, playful, anti-ornamental—that they tend to strip away one's assumptions about jewelry in the latter half of the 20ᵗʰ century, if not in the period before World War II." She was undoubtedly a star.

Her replacement at Boivin, Juliette Moutard, who designed the Boivin starfish, left a very different impression. Perhaps equally important to how the story is publicly perceived and understood, the Boivin archive, in contrast to Belperron's, has been kept mostly a secret, allowing for much conjecture and intrigue about the provenance of many designs and pieces. That seems to be exactly the way Nathalie Hocq, its current owner since 2000, wants to keep it. Hocq, a sixty-four-year-old uncommunicative beauty best known for her habit of smoking man-sized cigars and her former position as jewelry director of Cartier who inherited a Cartier fortune, is just another of the sphinxlike figures strewn along the path I followed into the history of the starfish.

The history of Boivin up until 1930, when Suzanne Belperron struck out on her own, merely explains the design environment that the starfish were conceived in. When the curtain rose on Paris in the 1930s, Boivin occupied a somewhat exalted position in the jewelry world. It had become a mecca for fashionable rich clients who wanted something beyond the flat black-and-white Art Deco pieces studded with diamonds that had dominated the prior decade. Jeanne, now sole proprietor, pushed her designs and salon in several directions. She moved Boivin from Rue des Pyramides to the

Palais-Royal on the Avenue de l'Opéra, a bold decision at a time
when most jewelers in Paris were establishing themselves in the
tonier Place Vendôme, a square in the First Arrondissement underneath a statue of Napoleon I in a Roman Senator—style toga that
would become a high-end shopping mecca. She had remarked while
hunting for a new space that she "did not want a boutique" for the
passing trade, one adorned with the silk, velvet, and wood paneling
that was typical décor for other jewelry stores at the time. Somewhat in contrast to her proper, discreet personal appearance and
manner, in the salon she opted for edginess. She hired a well-known
decorator, André Groult, her brother-in-law, to help with the design.[3] It was as if the Boivin salon were her plumage. She covered the
walls with straw marquetry that her last designer, Marie-Caroline
de Brosses, remembered, "shone like gold straw." White lead paint
gave an enameled appearance to an old dark wood fretwork display
cabinet. Overall, it was more rustic than other salons and that distinguished it from bourgeois fustiness. She burned sandalwood in-
cense. It was a maverick environment and backdrop for stones and
designs that were assertively unique. Modern. Cutting-edge. Boivin
attracted a clientele that wanted something new and different. The
new salon cemented the impression with an enviable array of artistic
patrons and style setters that included the painter Pierre Bonnard,
writer Colette, filmmaker Jean Cocteau, and composers Cole Porter
and Erik Satie, among notable others. The fashionable Lady Duff
Cooper and the Duchess of Windsor came to shop, as did European royalty. Then as now, celebrity style captured attention and
advertised the Boivin brand. Her clients found their way to her by
referral only.

Jeanne needed to replace Suzanne Belperron after her departure, and she decided on a very different designer, Moutard. Juliette was also malleable to Jeanne's specifications, an essential
requirement for working with Madame Boivin. She wasn't the
finger-popping, hot new talent that Belperron had been, nor as

headstrong. Moutard had designed small clocks before she went to work for Boivin. She was what was called a Raphaelite in her time, a reference to being of unspecific gender, like an angel. She was soft, whereas Belperron had been hard. Photos of her depict a plain-faced woman, unadorned and more coarsely featured than the elegant Belperron. Her operating style was more relaxed and easygoing than her predecessor's. She effusively talked over a design with Boivin clients, while Madame, a bit stern, stayed in the shadows. A former colleague of Belperron's told me a story that paints a picture of her I cannot shake. When showing gemstones to a client, she would extend her hand to show the stones cradled in her lengthy upturned fingernail, like a claw. The image, nearly grotesque, conveyed Belperron's strong sense of drama. Moutard, more measured and less flamboyant, as befitted a former clockmaker, put whatever flair she had into her designs.

Those designs were her hallmark. And she got along with Madame. The collaboration between Jeanne and Juliette was a fruitful one. It spawned the starfish. Madame Boivin not only ran the business but she usually had the brainstorm for the designs that were created at Boivin. Yet because she did not draw, she could only talk them through with her designers, who sometimes worked with a paintbox close at hand to render an idea on paper. Boivin biographer Françoise Cailles describes Jeanne Boivin's role as being like a sculptor or colorist. She had the big idea that she talked over with the designer. Then Juliette made the sketch, often in gouache from her paintbox while seated at her workbench, in a workshop behind the salon that was cramped with eighteen employees needed to fill thirty-three orders in 1933 alone. Boivin was booming.

And this is important: so confident were these women of the value and uniqueness of their designs that they continued the practice of the Belperron era of not signing their jewelry, and often did not keep drawings. A client's wishes were never written into the record books. Most clients gave up trying to influence a design since their comments were rarely taken into account. Boivin, Moutard, and Jeanne Boivin's daughter, Germaine, who had also entered the business with her mother, believed, arrogantly or wishfully, that their pieces were distinctive enough to not need written identification. Mostly, they were right. The problems this has caused for the chroniclers of Boivin and the story of the pieces they created were not their concern. However, their stance on the matter is confirmed by two unmistakable designs to emerge from Juliette's sketchbook, a chameleon created in 1939 and the iconic Boivin starfish.

We won't know what inspired Juliette Moutard to design the starfish. She played with the idea after Madame Boivin had brought a number of seashells into the salon. According to Marie-Caroline de Brosses, the last designer to work for Boivin before it shuttered its doors in 1992, Jeanne and her daughter, Germaine, often brought shells and bones, sometimes glued together, into the salon after walks or outings in nature. De Brosses considered the practice funny and a little odd, and guessed that it had always been the way Madame Boivin operated with her designers, suggesting a motif and prodding for its creation. Moutard's sketches, when they exist, typically say "from an idea of Madame Boivin." Animal motifs and a new naturalism began to be evident in Boivin designs from 1929 onward. From 1933 to 1935 a wave of shell designs from whelks to winged shells to ammonites made their way into the Boivin salon showroom. A Boivin diamond whelk brooch appeared on international socialite Mrs. Reginald Fellowes in a photo for *Vogue* in 1933. In 1934 there was a platinum and diamond starfish clip. And then, suddenly, a showstopper appeared in her sketchpad of cardboard and tracing paper. A cabochon ruby and amethyst pavé (from the French word meaning "to pave," for small stones set tightly together for continuous sparkle) starfish with rays that were articulated by twenty-eight yellow gold joints. As with many of the pieces to come from Boivin, once Juliette captured them on paper, Jeanne Boivin stayed away until they came back from the fabricator, ready to approve. It was a period of some suspense since the pressure to deliver the design—and these were complicated designs with moving parts—shifted onto the fabricator. Boivin's eminence in the trade depended both on design originality and the quality of its workmanship.

Boivin began to attract a clientele that was confident and brazen enough by the standards of the day to encourage designers to push the limits. There should be no doubt about the fact that Jeanne was an exacting taskmistress. Jeanne did not draw designs herself but made notes on the drawings made by her designers. She was a tireless perfectionist who wanted symmetry from every angle of a Boivin piece and on more than one occasion sent back to the workshop a whole order that she did not think was up to her standards. In one reported instance, her in-house workmaster, Robert Davière, burst into tears when Jeanne asked him to remount a stone for the third time.[4]

Jeanne Boivin's high card in the jewelry business had always been her relationship with a stable of workshop specialists. The making of a piece of jewelry was a collaboration far more complicated than I, or the woman who blithely selects a finished piece, can imagine. Juliette Moutard's sketch of starfish was sent out to one of Jeanne's favorite and best fabricators, Charles Profillet, the workmaster who made all three, and possibly a fourth, ruby and amethyst starfish. His minute initials can be seen with the aid of a jeweler's magnifying loupe on their undersides.

Jean Pierre Brun, whose family fabricated jewelry for generations and knew Charles Profillet, painted me a picture of what a puzzle a design with articulated pieces like the Boivin starfish could be for the fabricators who set them into gold. I imagined architects and contractors envisioning a skyscraper. The sheer challenge might have at first seemed insurmountable, but artisans accepted it as a test of skill and capability that could become a singular achievement.

Making gold jewelry is an ancient art and alchemy that dates back five thousand years to the sands of the Euphrates River, where gold was first discovered. To quantify and measure it, the ancients used barley grains or carob seeds (from which the word "carat" is derived) to balance and weigh it on a scale. They divided it into fractions of twenty-four, meaning that pure gold is twenty-four karats. Eighteen-karat gold, which was used for the starfish and most precious jewelry, is eighteen, indicating that the six remaining karats of weight (carob seeds balanced on the scale) were copper and nickel to be mixed with the molten gold to harden it and make it durable. Alloys could also affect color. Achieving the mix of copper and silver that would create a desired tint was another specialty of the goldsmith.

The process began with the goldsmith who melted the eighteen-karat gold ingots or grains into "their own soup," the alloy, to make the sheet of metal that was used, and ended with the lapidary who cut and set the stones. The raw gold and its recipe of alloys was first heated to its liquid state (1650 degrees Fahrenheit) in small crucibles placed in a furnace to liquefy before being poured into sheets to cool. Next came the magic step by the skilled craftsmen who gave a design, once a drawing on paper, its first real gold form. At this stage the collaboration between fabricator and designer was crucial. In gritty, wood-floored workshops filled with furnaces and men at workbenches with their sleeves rolled up working under table lamps, the starfish were truly made manifest.

The secretive craftsmen did not publicize their techniques, but the starfish were most likely to have been made by "chasing," gently hammering a specialized tool, a "punch," actually more like a stamp, to shape a sheet of eighteen-karat gold over a nickel or agate model. By the 1950s this step would be done in beeswax for the "lost wax" casting method, but the Boivin starfish were made without a mold in the 1930s. Another Frenchman, Sylvain Chervin of Carvin French Jewelers in New York, whose uncle André came to the United States from Paris in 1954 and has shared his history of the French jewelry trade with Sylvain, believes it more likely that the jeweler, in this case in a workshop that had a close relationship to the designer and knew from experience how to read her complex drawing, would have been able to manufacture the piece without a model. The fabricator would have formed the rays from a sheet of gold one at a time, then sliced through them to create the links for articulation. The pieces, like the hinged bones of a gold vertebra, were meticulously cleaned and refined by another specialist before they could be assembled. The jeweler's hand tools, little steel drills resembling modern dental drills and shaped steel blades called gravers, were used to smooth and chisel the settings for the 312 amethyst and ruby gemstones that were set by the stone setter in tandem with the lapidary who cut and shaped the stones—yet another pair of skilled hands in the process. Then the links, or joints, would be soldered or riveted together, much the way a gold bracelet or necklace is fashioned for flexibility. In either case, each step was performed by a specialist in his art. Madame Boivin had her own lapidary in-house, so it is possible that the last step in the completion of the starfish was added in the workroom behind the Boivin salon. I have heard several contemporary jewelers express wonder at exactly how the Boivin starfish was constructed and assembled. They consider it a miraculous piece of craftsmanship out of a bygone era. "It is a secret that is still held by the jeweler," according to Ulysses Dietz, chief curator and curator of decorative arts at the Newark Museum.

Madame Boivin, as was her practice, kept close watch over the process. She probably visited the Profillet workshop, two hundred

meters down the street from the Boivin salon, to check on how
the work was progressing. By then in her sixties, she often stayed
late in the salon, her years of nighttime soirees behind her.

The process was much like an assembly line in miniature, and one
assumes its tasks were performed expertly and proudly at every
stage. In one estimate, three hundred hours would have been spent
by another half-dozen specialists before it was completed. All this
was for *one* starfish. No wonder no two are exactly the same. Each
owner can bask in the satisfaction that her starfish is in some way
unique. With its hand-hewn irregularities and variations, each
piece is one of a kind. It must have been a moment of intense ex-
pectancy when designer and jeweler awaited the delivery and un-
veiling of the piece. Surely workmaster Charles Profillet's face was
flushed with pride and victory when he left his workshop on Rue
Chabanais, a backstreet behind the Louvre once known for its
famous high-end brothel, Le Chabanais (frequented by Edward
VII, Prince of Wales; Toulouse-Lautrec; Cary Grant; Humphrey
Bogart; Mae West; and diplomatic guests of the French government, but that's another story . . .)[5], and strode with the starfish
in his pocket to the nearby Boivin salon to present it to Madame
Boivin and Mademoiselle Moutard. *Voilà.*

Butterflies, horseheads, ladybugs, chameleons, lion claws, pigeon
wings, roosters, squirrels, turtles, and dragonflies emerged from
Juliette's sketchbook during the thirties and forties, yet it was the
starfish that remained one of Madame Boivin's most favorite pieces.
The starfish in particular, like inanimate puppets to emerge from
a carpenter's bench, were about to be dispersed onto two conti-
nents, pinned on the shoulders and busts of some of the most
beautiful and fashionable women in the world at the time, to
begin their journey from then to now. In time, they became, according to Cailles, "Boivin's most famous creation: the starfish."

It was Madame Boivin's favorite from the start, perhaps the reason that one version was seemingly kept by Boivin until it was offered for sale in Geneva in 2006. It landed in the hands of another Hollywood actress, this one spirited enough to buy it on a payment plan, and is still described by the American Jewelry University, an online encyclopedia, as "the most famous and iconic of Boivin's pieces."

The hubris that led these designing women to refuse to sign their work was admirable on one hand. I liked their confidence and pluck, but the practice has surely permitted a mind-boggling tangle of doubts, deceptions, and confusions to arise. (How such hauteur would challenge our label-conscious fashion world today!) On one hand Jeanne Boivin did not want to sign Boivin pieces because she believed the design alone was adequate to identify them. "From 1930 onwards it becomes extremely difficult to identify with precision the author of any jewel which left the Avenue de l'Opéra workshop . . . the final realization was invariably a joint effort . . . That is how they wanted it," explains Françoise Cailles in her book about Boivin. Yet the practice of authentication of such pieces invariably requires mention of whether or not they were signed and is relied upon by auctioneers and dealers. I had also been told that signage was sometimes removed from fine jewelry to avoid taxes and customs regulations. And then I had heard also that jewelers had on occasion taken a piece they believed to be Boivin to be stamped on its underside, so that prospective buyers would have confidence in its origin. (And thus establishing that it was possibly *not* original!) What was I to make of this? Like so much of the jewelry business it was shrouded in ambiguity and it would plague my attempt to identify the starfish later.

Chapter Eight

WAS ANXIOUS TO MEET JANET ZAPATA, A JEWELRY EXPERT who had helped Lee Siegelson and other leading jewelers research some of the famous vintage items they advertised for sale. A writer herself, she produced the text that described the provenance and history of starfish and other pieces in catalogues and online notices. As an independent scholar and museum consultant, Zapata had written books about jewelry and curated exhibitions. When I had asked Lee Siegelson how he knew the starfish he offered for sale was the third one made by Boivin, he told me to "ask Janet."

Major jewelers rested their credibility and reputations on people like Janet, but they were seldom visible. She, and a few others like her, moved about the jewelry sales world at will, and as I would learn, usually had up-to-the-minute information about pieces that came on the market. I was prepared to value her as someone who, like an academic in other disciplines, was more interested in learning things about the pieces that are being sold than in sales or client relationships.

The woman who met me for tea at the Cosmopolitan Club on the Upper East Side of New York was a neatly dressed middle-aged woman with short brown hair. Her shoes were sensible low heels. I got the impression she was at home in her own skin, and she was confident enough to be open in her professional capacity. There was no need to dance around the subject of the starfish. We plunged right into it.

She had first seen a starfish in 2007 with Lee Siegelson, whose acquisitions she often researched, she said.[1] She believed Claudette Colbert's was the first one made by Boivin in Paris. Then Millicent's was the second. Lee had also owned the third. "Jewelry gets stuck in vaults," she explained. Dealers wait patiently for certain pieces to make an appearance on the market. The characteristic that distinguished the starfish for her, among the many pieces of jewelry that she has studied and observed, was simple. "These pieces move. They are not stationary. They are big and their design came up through the Art Deco period. In the thirties there was a figural change that they were part of," she said, offering her grounded understanding of the starfish's appeal. "Jewelry became an art form in that period." She added that the later ones, those extra two or three that were made in the eighties and nineties, "they were the same design but stiffer." One that came up for sale at Christie's that had belonged to the designer Oscar de la Renta was a "later one." She told me that if I saw one I would know the difference. It was more than just a matter of size, even though the newer ones were a few centimeters bigger than the originals. I must have looked dubious. "You'll just know," she assured me.

I could see that unlike the dealers I had spoken with so far, Janet's attachment to the pieces we were discussing was much more objective. She did not have the passionate personal connection to the pieces or get the same buzz from having them around her that the dealers did. She mentioned how she had watched dealers, especially the men, fall in love with jewelry. "They love their work. Unlike all the other decorative arts, you touch and wear jewelry. It becomes part of you. You can hold it and carry it. There is no big box." She went a step further, hypothesizing that the attachment men have to jewelry often substitutes for extramarital intrigue. "Men in the jewelry world don't cheat. They relate to women differently. As experts. The jewelry is what is always there the next day for them," she said. "You can put it in your pocket and touch it. That is what is so special." And the chase never ends.

When I asked for her overview of the jewelry business in general, she was quick to answer. "Everyone has a secret. The jewelry business is very secretive, what they have and who they know. To be a dealer, you have to have a lot, a lot of money. They control it. They buy and sell jewelry every day, and because of the money, it is very secretive." She explained that every shop was somewhat in hostage to "the money people," either partners, lenders, or banks. "The dealers in those stores own a percentage but not usually all," she said. There were "upstairs jewelers," like Siegelson and Verdura and "money people," in the parlance of the industry. I assumed that Siegelson, because of what I had heard about the fortune he had inherited from his father's diamond business, fit both models.

She told me a little self-deprecating story when we talked about the kind of women who wear Boivin starfish brooches. "They usually have vast wealth and are women who are self-assured and out at all events. As you grow into your personality, your jewelry gets bigger. All have important jewelry. Other people just get more diamonds, which is not the same thing as a starfish. It takes a sophisticated someone who has an eye to go into this. The average person wouldn't want to buy a starfish or understand it. It's too threatening." Where did she fit into this? I asked her. Again she laughed. When she worked at Tiffany, she said, her employer had called her in at one point and said that she was a "little jewelry" person. The big pieces, like the starfish, were not her own style.

I told Janet that I would soon need to go to Paris and London to delve further into the starfish history. She mentioned several people whom I should speak with. I could see the wheels turning in her mind. "Tell them you talked to Janet and perhaps they can help you figure out the puzzle." That was what attracted her to this line of work. The puzzle.

I had heard that Audrey Friedman, a principal with Primavera Gallery in Chelsea, was an expert on Boivin. When I e-mailed her we agreed to meet at the fine art and jewelry show at the Park Avenue Armory, where Primavera had a booth. As I approached the Primavera booth, I knew that the woman with jet-black hair, dark lipstick, and white skin as smooth as porcelain with a large Alexander Calder pin on her black dress had to be Audrey Friedman. There was something very ladylike and old-world about her on one hand and modern and savvy on the other. Phlegmatic now, after forty years Audrey knows her business from both sales experience and tireless research. She writes about and lectures on French jewelry from the 1930s and 1940s. "One of the reasons for the superior workmanship of French jewelry was the apprenticeship system, whereby a person would begin to learn his trade at age fourteen. This gave rise to a class of jeweler who was skilled in all aspects of jewelry work to a degree almost unknown today, and it is one of the things that made French jewelry so special," she told me. It was the design and craftsmanship that attracted her. The Primavera Web site boldly asserts, "We are not interested in large diamonds or masses of precious stones—this, for us, is geology rather than jewelry. We are interested in great style, exciting design, and integrity of workmanship." Design, not rocks.

She lamented the end of the days when "you could find Boivin and other pieces from this period because other dealers didn't know what they were. Nobody was paying attention." But Boivin has been in demand again recently, she reported. And Boivin pieces are harder to find. "The dealers are gone. There used to be ten dealers on Rue Saint-Honoré in Paris," she said. Now there are perhaps two. The starfish appeal, in her opinion, to the same people who wanted them in the 1940s. "Sophisticated women with money. Their appeal is visual and feminine."

The business of buying jewelry like the Boivin starfish has always been based, in her experience, on one criterion. "Does the piece make your heart beat faster?" She said that she had been caught by this herself. A woman dealer can more easily flaunt her wares by wearing them. A Boivin bracelet, the Alexander Calder pin she wore when I met her at the Armory show, and other favorite pieces have become part of her private collection. "My heart often beats fast, that's when I have to have it." She laughed. "If I wanted pieces that we acquired, I kept them. It has always been about the piece for me." She added regretfully, "Unfortunately, it becomes about the money. It is so expensive these days that you have to sell them." But the sale, even of an expensive piece that makes a profit, can generate a sense of loss. "I miss knowing I have it," she said, smiling. I heard the echo of Russell Zelenetz and Stephen Feuerman telling me they liked having the necklace around that the buyer didn't claim. "When you have them you connect with the spirit of the maker. Like listening to music," she added. Abiding affection for what they do seemed to distinguish and unite jewelers as a class. Most will tell you that they can't imagine doing anything else, or like Audrey, they tried other professions and gave them up.

We were sitting in the Primavera gallery in Chelsea late in the afternoon while the winter sun went down over the Hudson River out the window. The lights in the Art Deco lamps on display around the gallery came up and threw their warm glow around us. She and her husband and business partner, Haim Manishevitz, who had sat quietly in the back while Audrey and I talked, joined in to tell me the story of a male client who bought jewelry for his wife. "In one case we suspected that when the wife of the man who bought a piece was away he put it on and walked around the house." Audrey chuckled.

Chapter Nine

THE WORLD OF FINE JEWELRY, I WAS ABOUT TO LEARN, is full of contradictions. So dazzlingly cosmopolitan seen through the windows of Fifth Avenue showrooms and jewelry stores in most major cities, it is a swashbuckling frontier in the back rooms and exchanges where fine jewelry deals are struck and fortunes are lost or made. Like most true businesses that traffic in style, it relies on artifice and operates on grit. Jewelers re-create themselves and forge fresh images, as had Murray Mondschein. I kept on, tracking down figures in the jewelry world who could help me understand the mysteries of the starfish and lead me to their current owners. They were a marvelously varied lot.

When I called the Fred Leighton salon, now owned by the hundred-year-old diamond company Kwiat, and asked for Murray,

I was advised to call Pat Saling. All queries for Murray these days, since Kwiat purchased Fred Leighton, must be made through Saling, a colleague of Murray's for more than twenty-two years. Saling, who now steers her own company, Pat Saling, for fine estate and precious jewelry, also has the dubious honor of being the gatekeeper for her old boss. "Murray says he doesn't really know anything about the starfish," she told me when I first called. But when I persisted in asking to make a date with him, at least to hear his overview of the market for such pieces, she scheduled an appointment for me a month later. I traveled to be in New York that day and began early at Verdura, perusing old *Vogue* and *Harper's Bazaar* editions with jewelry features and advertisements alongside Caroline Stetson, a Verdura staffer. When it was time to leave, I told her that I had an appointment with Murray. Ward Landrigan, standing within earshot, raised his eyebrows. "You do? That's great. That should be interesting," he chimed in, typically enthusiastic. I was no sooner down on Fifth Avenue than my cell phone rang and it was an assistant in Pat's office telling me that Murray was not in town and unable to keep our appointment. My attempts to make another date with him were fruitless. I was told that I would have to "call Pat." Later that day after several visits to other jewelers, I ran into Caroline Stetson on the street who told me she had just passed Murray at the corner stoplight.

I made yet another date with Murray that was canceled and I was again told that he had nothing to say about the starfish. I didn't wholly give up on him but I figured that I might have to settle for interviewing Pat if she would talk to me. She knew a lot about Murray and his business after their long working relationship.

Pat Saling's office was on the fifth floor of a modern no-frills building on Forty-eighth Street off Fifth Avenue, the dividing line between the glitzy retailers and the gritty diamond dealers. There was no storefront, no sign, no indication of a major jewelry dealer's headquarters though her Web site touts "fine estate and precious jewelry." Her own office was unpretentious—drab, even—with a print of two winged cherubs playing the mandolin, a familiar image from greeting cards and valentines, hung crookedly on the desk behind her. The one high window was in need of washing. Obviously, business was conducted there, not marketing or showbiz. Men in aprons, jewelers one supposes, came and went through a doorway on the opposite wall. "What can I do for you?" asked Pat from the other side of her black leather desk, obviously a bit put out by my insistence on speaking to her or Murray. Heavyset, dressed all in black, and sporting a big emerald ring, she was both formidable and a bit refreshing. She did not try to impress.

I told her I had heard that Murray made reproductions of the starfish in the 1980s. "They're not called reproductions," she told me sternly, bristling at the term. "That's David Webb. He reproduces," she said, invoking a name I would hear again. "Look, everybody stole something from everybody in this business. It's not rocket science. You create demand in this business . . . Jacques Bernard tried to do this with Boivin in the 1980s." I was having to read between the lines there, but I deciphered later that she might have been telling me Murray made some of the starfish with the last director of Boivin, Jacques Bernard, in the 1980s.

"Murray doesn't think he can help you. We're just merchants," she explained, suggesting that all this interest in the starfish and their dealers was a bit overheated, in her opinion. She explained that she had been in the business since 1978, and, "Yes, there were great designs, but the end result is to sell something. And there is not an emphasis on brooches today." She told me she had diamond orchids, violets, lions, and starfish that she thinks are more delectable than the Boivin starfish. She unlocked and opened the safe next to her desk to show me a diamond orchid. But had she seen a starfish? I asked. She breezed along. "Millicent's was beat-up.

We made an offer. There was a broker, no dealing direct. That's not the same. We all share clients in this business. Sometimes it takes six months to make an offer." She told me that in the 1980s, Oscar Heyman kept Diana Vreeland's Maltese cross Verdura bracelet in a safe for years before selling it, to illustrate how sometimes it takes a long period of time to find the right market for a vintage piece. It is an example of the phenomenon that Janet Zapata had explained to me, when "the upstairs money people" are jewelers with pockets so deep that they can afford to invest in six- or sometimes seven-figure pieces and hold on to them for a decade or longer while they appreciate in value.

Until that moment I did not know that the Rogers starfish had been shopped to Saling. "We all saw it," she sniffed. "Sam wanted a hundred thousand extra." I took this to mean that Sam Loxton at Lucas Rarities in London had shown it around to New York dealers with his markup before it sold to Lee Siegelson. Obviously, she had passed on the chance to buy it. I was reminded how small this world of New York jewelers is.

Hard-nosed and practical, Saling provided a good contrast to the dewier, more romantic notions about the starfish, though I suspect she is as enthusiastic and addicted to the business as almost every other dealer I have spoken with. "Nobody starts out to be in the jewelry business. We all just washed up on this shore," she said. "It is a constant treasure hunt your whole life." She was introduced to the business without the family connections that many jewelers have, she explained. She came from a family of social workers, but when she worked at an antiques show in Hackensack, New Jersey, her three-week stint at selling jewelry grew to five years. For a while she worked in a pawnshop "where a pass-through loan on gemstones was a dollar a point." I didn't understand it all, but I got the picture. When I investigated later, I learned that a carat, in describing a stone, is not a size but a weight measure. Each one-hundredth of it is a point. A ten-pointer's pawn value was ten dollars. A carat was one hundred dollars, and so on. "There was a strict code of ethics. You were given handshakes and words, no contracts. My brother, a banker, was horrified," she said, laughing. But she explained that "if you do not honor your word one time, there is no next time." She went to work with Murray Mondschein for a month and ended up staying twenty-one years, mostly running the shop at Fred Leighton while he traveled eight months of the year, she told me. She vividly remembered when she was twenty-seven years old in the 1970s, being summoned at 5 A.M. by Imelda Marcos. "Mam would like to see some jewelry," the caller from Imelda's said, and Pat took some pieces to show her, accessing the security to the Marcos's apartment and standing guard over her jewelry as the shoulder-high safe was opened. Marcos, wife of the president of the Philippines at the time, became infamous for her lavish spending. She owned twelve hundred pairs of shoes, but her jewelry collection, often compared to a royal family's collection by the press, was also excessive.

The jewelry business is a calling, offered Pat. "It's a journey, you grow into it." She remembered the 1980s. "Back then it was about how to find the dollars to buy the jewelry. Now we have the money but there aren't as many pieces left to buy," she said, giving me a hint as to why the Boivin starfish have increased in value over the last twenty years. I asked her to explain the starfish's value to me.

"You know when you hold the starfish what it is. There are no catches, is the first thing. It's smooth. You have to turn it over and look at it. You can't see this from a book because a picture isn't three-dimensional. Boivin was a designer with a sense of design and good craftsmen. Cartier made junk."

She was relaxing, a little less prickly. "We sold a couple of starfish in the eighties. I know I sold one in 1980." She can't be sure, she says, whether it was old or new. I was careful not to interrupt with too many questions. "Claudia Cohen's must have been bought from us," she said, mentioning the starfish that had belonged to the late New York celebrity and social journalist for Fox News who was married to billionaire Ron Perelman. "Now *he's* a piece of work," she added, in a rare aside about a client. She continued to tell me that in 2012 she sold a starfish made in the 1980s, one of "the later ones." In spite of professing ignorance and having nothing to say about the starfish, she seemed quite a compendium of their New York sales history. Then as quickly as she had opened to me, like one of the jeweled flowers in her safe, she closed her petals and snapped shut. Our conversation about the starfish was over.

On the street, I allowed myself a moment of cynicism over the terminology jewelers used when someone made a piece that was just like a famous piece and quietly put it on the market, which is what I gathered Murray had done. Saling had admonished me for calling them "reproductions." I gathered that "copy" was not an allowed term, either. So what was the permitted description? "Fake"? or maybe "ripoff"? The ethics of the business certainly got a little squishy when it came to dealing with new versions. They would remain "reproductions" to me.

I was back on Forty-eighth Street several months later. A museum curator friend of mine who once worked for Doyle, the family-owned auction and appraisal house in New York, suggested I speak with her former colleague Berj Zavian. Berj had risen to national fame in recent years appearing on the *Antiques Roadshow* television program as the silver-haired straight-talking appraiser. He was a bit gruff when I spoke with him on the phone but he agreed to meet with me in New York. It was a cold January day when I walked down Fifth Avenue from Fifty-seventh Street, past the big showy retail jewelry stores like Harry Winston, Van Cleef & Arpels, Tiffany & Co., and Cartier, all of them open to "foot traffic," and crossed over to Forty-eighth Street on the west side. I marveled at how the world changes immensely in those nine blocks. Forty-eighth Street is in the diamond district, and the street was bustling with Orthodox Jews in long dark coats, ear muffs under their brimmed fedoras or Cossack hats that wintry morning. The entrance of the building where Cluster Jewelry, Berj's business, is located had men in groups, mostly Hispanic, placing bets on card games on the sidewalk while they waited to load and unload the vans and armored cars at the curbs. Their breath rose like steam in the cold air as they rolled dollies stacked with boxes up ramps and over curbs. The lighting in the lobby was watery and the men who huddled in the elevator with me made no eye contact, especially the Hasidim, whose religious rules make them uneasy mingling with or talking to strange women. Most, I figured, were delivering jewels to the craftsmen on the floors above. The smell of Chinese food from the restaurant next door seemed to fill the pale green hallways. Everything felt secretive, dark, Middle Eastern. Cluster Jewelry, with its lathes and tools in the entry vestibule, was clearly a workshop. Berj's daughter Robin sat at the stool behind the counter, stringing pearls. She wore an oversized orange Nike T-shirt. She had warned me to come promptly because she wanted to leave early to practice for the upcoming Super Bowl halftime show she would be performing in the following weekend.

When I arrived Berj had stepped out, but by the time I got my coat off and was ready to ask questions, he returned. I wasn't certain it was him for a minute. He looked nothing like the sleek silver-haired man on *Antiques Roadshow.* This man was wearing sneakers and a soiled jeweler's apron. He had a magnifying loupe on a string around his neck. His nails were long and yellow. He also ignored me. He went back into the shop and started to eat his lunch out of a Styrofoam box. I had to yell to make conversation with him. "Why should I talk to you?" he shouted. I told him again about the book I was writing. He asked if I had a gemology degree. I did not, I told him. He instructed me to go and get one and then come back to see him. I watched Robin carefully. Her eyelids did not flicker. Then he asked me if I would pay him ten percent of my earnings on the book. I didn't think he was serious. I told him he might be surprised how little that would be. I decided to ignore this scattershot banter and keep asking questions. He answered me with curt yeses and nos. "Maybe I saw a starfish," he conceded. Then I asked how he got into the jewelry business.

His father taught him, he explained. He had learned from his brother. Those siblings had been born in Baghdad. Berj's father came to the United States when he was five years old and his older brother was eleven. This story was coming from a man who was talking at me but sitting at a workbench almost out of sight behind shelves, across the room. "Do you want rice?" Robin asked him, interrupting. He complained that his crown had fallen off a tooth and that his hip hurt. Then he swerved back into the subject. "Most jewelers can't sit at the bench," said Berj. "You learn about a piece at the bench." I understood that he was talking about actually making jewelry and that he was proud of his prowess in the trade. I asked how long it would have taken to make a Boivin starfish. He didn't hesitate to venture that it probably took two to three weeks.

He asked if I knew who David Webb was. I said I did not. "You don't know who David Webb is?" he repeated, incredulous. David Webb had been a quintessential American jeweler on Fifty-seventh Street in New York for sixty-seven years. Jackie Kennedy, Diana Vreeland, Liz Taylor, the Duchess of Windsor all wore Webb creations that have often appeared in the pages of *Vogue* and other style magazines. Berj said that his father had sold gemstones to Webb. He explained that from 1936 to 1948 his father, who by then was a platinum dealer, got into the costume jewelry field and "made a fortune." The Cluster Jewelry company repairs jewelry, some real, some reproductions, and does custom work for clients today. By this time Berj had come forward to speak to me from across the counter. I hoped I was making progress. He said he had seventy-two rings in the jewelry case between us. When he pulled out a selection to show me I reached out to touch one. "Don't touch," he said, looking up at me under bushy white brows. I imagined that I had broken some part of jewelry-world protocol, touching the objects uninvited, which reminded me how special the invitation at Verdura to hold a starfish had been. I withdrew my hand and apologized.

I asked again if he had ever seen a starfish. "I might of," he said. He said he knew Joan Crawford had had one. She did not as far as I knew, but I did not correct him. Perhaps he confused her with Claudette Colbert. He told me that Doris Day had been known for keeping the clothes and jewelry that she wore in her movie roles. He told me how Tiffany had gotten into the jewelry business. When he was a manufacturer of paper and then glass shades, Louis Comfort Tiffany learned that Empress Eugénie in Paris was selling off her possessions in Europe. Tiffany went to buy from her with $5 million he acquired from a backer. When he came back and showed his Fourteenth Street financial partner the jewelry he had, his partner said, "We're not in the jewelry business." So Louis got his financing from friends and the rest of Tiffany & Co.'s successful growth story is history.

I asked Berj if he knew Lee Siegelson. "His dad was a gangster," he said matter-of-factly. I had heard that the late elder Siegelson had been a tough-minded diamond merchant. Berj had his opinions of everyone. When I first called him he had suggested Susan Abeles, the director of U.S. jewelry at Bonhams in New York. He said she was someone who knew jewelry history and

with whom I should speak. Trying to steer the conversation back
to the starfish, I mentioned Abeles. "I taught her. I picked her out
of the silver department," he told me with evident pride.

I knew that Berj knew a lot about jewelry history, even though at
the moment he was playing the part of a simple jewelry maker at
his bench. But he couldn't help himself. I felt like we were having
more of a boxing match than a conversation. One moment he
would feign ignorance and humility. The next his wealth of knowledge would take over. He told me he had spent thirty-seven years
working in auction houses. He was an expert on South American
amethysts. The Boivin starfish have amethysts, I interjected, but
he said he didn't know anything about those. He also said he knew
a lot about Ceylon rubies. I mentioned that the starfish had Bur-
mese rubies. He shrugged. "Women used to wear these pieces on
fur coats when they went for lunch at Lindy's," he said. "They
hung their coats on hooks at the door." The carefree, careless image of well-dressed women flinging furs with big jeweled brooches
onto hooks by a doorway without worrying that they would be
stolen lingers in my mind. It was truly a simpler time to be a rich
woman.

It seemed Berj didn't have much more to add about the starfish. I put on my coat to leave. Neither he nor Robin said good-
bye when I hollered my thanks and said I'd be in touch. I left past
the OXYGEN IN USE sign in the hallway. A pile of cardbord boxes
was being loaded onto dollies downstairs next to the messengers'
chained bikes. There were signs of industry, not style, everywhere
I turned. The contrast with Tiffany & Co., Cartier, Harry Winston, and Van Cleef & Arpels a few blocks uptown was daunting
at first, yet I was beginning to understand that gemstones and
shared history were links in the glittering chain that bound these
two worlds like a pair of sisters. One was posh and glamorous,
the other more humble, but they shared the same roots and

trafficked in the same wares. They could also disorient the public when they switched costumes and roles.

I believed that Berj, while ornery and difficult with me, had been honest. I don't think he knew much about the Boivin starfish, though I guessed he had seen one or two go past when he worked for auction houses. Few dealers could resist telling that they had admired the piece if they had seen it for themselves. I bundled up and readied to walk across the Fifth Avenue line to see James Givenchy. Yes, I thought, I should have known who David Webb was.

I had begun to notice that James Givenchy and his salon, Taffin, were frequently mentioned among young jewelers and in jewelry blogs. A woman I knew in Paris, who knew all the old players in the French and American business, told me she would "kill to meet James Givenchy." So I decided to call him.

The Taffin salon on Fifty-fourth Street off Fifth Avenue came as a surprise. Located on the fourth floor of a contemporary brick-and-glass building, it is not open to street trade. The sleek, well-lit showroom with a view onto the buildings across the street smacked of modernity and style. James's ornate French provincial desk sat across from a seating area for clients with a coral linen couch flanked by low shiny black tables arranged on a sisal rug. The mood was warm and sophisticated. James's refreshingly open personality and Taffin's cozy sophistication were a welcome contrast to my morning at Cluster.

Fair-haired and in his early fifties, Givenchy seemed downright boyish, wearing chinos and a zip-neck sweater. His casual appearance and perfect manners were disarmingly French to me, though he is a totally Americanized designer. "Jewelry is much more than the pieces it is made of. Part of its appeal is the people who have worn it before," he observed, giving credence to the notion that had inspired my interest in the Boivin starfish to begin with. He volunteered to help me. He was hopeful that Simon Teakle, a former head of jewelry for Christie's in New York, would know something of the starfish.

I phoned Simon Teakle the same day. The Simon Teakle Fine Jewelry store in Greenwich, Connecticut, known for estate and vintage collectibles, is open to the public without appointment. Its dapper owner, a former British gemologist, embodies the jeweler who is always on the prowl for the rare and beautiful. He had a reputation for the spring and energy of the hunter. He was extraordinarily responsive when I called and mentioned that James Givenchy had given me his name. "Yes, yes." He told me he had seen a Boivin starfish. He had sold one at Christie's auction house probably fifteen years ago. Finally, a bit of evidence, defining a trail. The 1996 sale that he spoke of began to ring a bell. I had seen the record of a sale in that year in Lotfinder, the online locator records from Christie's. At last I was starting to be able to make some connections between the sales histories dealers spoke of and a few owners who had come forward to speak with me.

Auction houses, especially Christie's, provide the best record of jewelry sales. Catalogues and online services such as Lotfinder are available to the public and are generally counted on to guarantee authenticity of the pieces that are offered for sale. Yet I was soon to learn that advertisement and the public record do not mean that it is any easier to find out where a piece of jewelry that is for sale came from or who bought it after the sale. The auction world operates with a more stylized version of the opacity I had encountered from dealers. It specializes in faux transparency.

It was another winter morning when I went to visit Daphne Lingon, a senior vice president and jewelry specialist at Christie's in New York City. Several dealers spoke highly of her and suggested that I consult with her about the starfish. She had, during her nineteen years at Christie's, organized auctions for Rockefeller heirs, Lauren Bacall, and the record-breaking sale of Liz Taylor's jewelry. I gathered when I telephoned Daphne to explain myself and make an appointment that she was dubious about speaking with me. When I called to confirm our date, she reminded me that she did not expect to discuss any of the general things we had talked about before. I was forewarned that she had a bit of an attitude. I would be careful to not waste her time with general questions about the jewelry business or the starfish.

When I arrived at Christie's in Rockefeller Center, I was escorted from the reception to the tightly secured jewelry business floors. Daphne's assistant guided me down the muted corridors to her office, but because other business was being conducted there, Daphne asked me to follow her to a plain uncluttered cubicle down the hall. A pale-skinned dark brunette, she had a plush lavender cashmere pashmina tied loosely around her neck. She wore high heels. The long wild hair, the heels, and her feminine clothes added up to a softly pretty presence, but the studious black-framed glasses that she wore lent her a strictly business air. We started cordially.

I knew that the machinations that move a piece of fine jewelry like the starfish from a family who has held it for years to the current marketplace, like Christie's, are simple and typically begin humbly. Families don't want to attract attention and they usually start the process of selling tentatively, to test the waters. Ward Landrigan had told me that clients had walked into Verdura carrying a dozen fine heirloom pieces in a paper bag. He recalled two sisters from Philadelphia who brought him fifteen pieces of jewelry that way on the train to New York. "Cloth-coat types," he remembered. Another client who had carried her jewelry in a paper bag had gone shopping at Pratesi and left the bag on the floor. Ward had helped her recover it.

Daphne had similar tales to tell. "People can just walk in with jewelry," she said, and shared the story of a woman who dropped in to Christie's from her morning jog with a seventeen-carat diamond bracelet that she had been meaning to get an estimate on. "She just didn't know its worth," she explained. A $1.5 million Kashmir sapphire came through the door with an unsuspecting owner not too long before. Pieces, even rare fine pieces, often make their way to auctions or estate dealers without a lot of fanfare. Old family pieces come up after any of the three *d*s: debt, divorce, death. Often the owners, and sometimes the dealers, don't know the real value of the jewelry until it is sold. What she didn't mention, and I was yet to learn, was that reproduction jewelry, whatever you want to call it, typically enters the market through auctions. Auctioneers, like dealers, are punctilious about not revealing where items for sale come from, and sometimes the history or catalogue copy about them is vague.

Daphne elaborated on the rarity of a Boivin starfish. "There are not so many things in the jewelry market that there are so few of. If you want a five- or ten-carat diamond, they are readily available," she said. "But there are very few starfish and a collector must wait until one comes up for sale." There is no way to know when that might be. Did she think there were more than three? I asked. She gave me an unknowing shrug. But significantly, she volunteered what I was just learning. "Not all of them are old. Maybe a handful are recirculated, reconsigned. You ask yourself, 'was that the one?'" This had the same effect on me as Russell Zelenetz's comment that there could be five starfish. It made me queasy.

Daphne directed me to Christie's Web site and said that the record of sales on Lotfinder and Artfacts were the best she could do to help me discover the history of a piece. Surely there was someone in-house who could remember the 2006 and 2008 sales whom I could speak to? I asked. I saw my query move across her expressive face. I imagined that she would like to help me and I got the impression that she knew who this person would be, but it was against policy to tell or help. She is disciplined. She was sorry, she said. I asked her to consider letting me speak with someone else. How can it be so sensitive to discuss wonderful pieces of jewelry that were made seventy-five years ago and sold ten, fifteen, and twenty years ago? I prodded her. The corner of her mouth twitched and she looked down. She was either amused or thought I was an idiot. Maybe both.

She reminded me that like dealers, auction houses do not reveal their consignors or buyers. For a brief moment I also saw a trace of conflict, that she would like to help. She said that she would speak with someone else in the department on my behalf; she was not hopeful. But there was one thing she could do to help me, she said coolly.

I could write a letter, a to-whom-it-may-concern variety, that explained my purpose and the book I was writing about the Boivin ruby and amethyst starfish brooches. Christie's would, from its records, forward it along to the parties who have bought the starfish over the years. But that would be the end of it. Either the buyers decided to respond to me on their own or they did not. I could not know their names or follow up with them directly. Christie's would not lobby on my behalf. It was one shot in the dark. Of course, I agreed.

I knew that this effort might not amount to much, but I was delighted to leave Christie's offices with something hopeful, finally. I almost, but not quite, bounded out into the snowy day like a happy puppy.

Chapter Ten

ON ANOTHER SNOWY DAY IN NEW MEXICO SEVERAL months later a happy surprise awaited me when I checked my e-mail messages. "Dear Cherie, your letter has arrived and yes I do own a starfish brooch which my husband purchased. I am happy to speak with you about it." She included her phone number and closed, "I would like to hear more about your project and perhaps we can meet. Best, Susan." I was flooded with an almost eerie sense of relief. It had seemed like an eternity since I had trusted Christie's to put out my letter of inquiry to the clients whom they knew had bought the starfish. The effort had seemed an empty black hole until that moment.

After all the cagey dealers and byzantine conversations I had had speaking with people in the jewelry business, those plain, direct words, "I do own a starfish," had fresh significance for me. Only once we spoke by phone did I detect the slight remnant of a Southern accent that would later help explain Susan Rotenstreich's friendly and open demeanor. Her name was familiar. It would turn out that we had actually met years before when our children attended the same school in Manhattan.

She gladly shared the story of acquiring and owning her starfish. Her husband had given the starfish to her as an anniversary present in the 1990s. She was a jewelry designer herself at the time. Some of her designs had been photographed and featured in major fashion magazines, but she left the business "when everyone and their daughter was getting into it. It wasn't a place for me," she explained. But her eye for fine jewelry remained specific and refined. Her husband, Jon W. Rotenstreich, principal of the Bayer Properties holding company, had seen the starfish at a preview for an upcoming Christie's auction. "Jon just loved it," explained Susan. They had talked about it, so it wasn't a total surprise when several weeks later he presented it to her in a box with a bow in the dressing room of their Park Avenue apartment as she dressed to go out to dinner. "I loved it," she remembered, her voice rising dramatically. That night she pinned it on her dress and wore it out.

Susan had seen a lot of jewelry as a designer and collector, but what struck her when she first saw the starfish was its articulation. "I so admired the design mechanism. I always checked out magazine and jewelry collections. But this was unique. I knew it was just beautiful and very special." Just the same, it is a challenging piece to wear and she admitted she had worn it only "from time to time." Its size and weight make it a difficult piece to wear. "It's heavy and you can't wear it if the fabric is too thin to balance it," she said almost apologetically. Susan wears it on a silk dress or a suit for an occasion such as her birthday or a night at the opera "when you want to feel sort of special," but she added that she had worn it most successfully on a gold chain at her neck with an open-collared white shirt. I have tried to envision this, since the starfish I have seen is large enough to span a woman's clavicle, but I assume she can bring it off.

I was reminded that fashionable Parisian women in the first decade of the twentieth century imaginatively found ways to pile on as much jewelry as possible when they stepped out in the evening. Some hung chokers on sautoirs or strings of pearls, donned bracelets on every arm and rings on almost every finger. For the inventive and spirited woman, brooches offered a realm of possibilities; they could adorn the flap of an evening bag or, as *Vogue* had illustrated in 1937, a hat. A stiffly fitted bodice or starchy lapel would fade from fashion, but one's jewels could be reincarnated.[1]

As a brooch Susan finds her starfish looks best on a cream-colored crepe de chine dress rather than on black, and because of its size and brightness she only pairs it with pearl earrings, "which don't compete with it." It cannot be worn casually. Susan and Jon are frequently photographed at charitable benefits and parties, in which the diminutive Susan is easy to spot. Her flair tends to arty, often turquoise jewelry, perhaps a pattern-appliquéd jacket. Though she told me she cannot recall being photographed with the starfish, there is a photo of her in 2008 at the Lincoln Center Fall Gala in New York City wearing it on a red dress under a black sweater jacket. The starfish is not wholly visible, partly obscured by her black wrap.

The brooch attracts attention, which is one reason to wear it sparingly. She mentioned security concerns. It is a hard piece not to notice—or forget. "People always say, oh that's pretty, or, that's unusual." The truth is, "One doesn't wear brooches very much anymore," she concluded. Most people don't really know how to deal with a jeweled sea creature the size of a hand. The people it attracts, she noted, are those "with a discerning eye for jewelry."

Her own daughter, now in her thirties, has shown no interest in it. "She'll inherit it and love it or put it up for auction," Susan said, laughing. It doesn't matter to her. Meanwhile the starfish is kept in a safe with the rest of her collection.

When the Boivin starfish first came up in my conversation with Sarah Davis at Siegelson, she told me it was likely that the designer had cleverly distinguished each starfish from the others by turning up two different rays on each one. If you numbered each of the rays, or arms, from one to five clockwise with number one pointed up at the top, the combinations would vary. Two and five, one and three, or one and four, and so on. When she said this I thought it would be easy to know which starfish was which. Every time I saw a photograph of one in a jeweler's advertisement or auction catalogue I quickly looked to see which rays were flipped slightly at their tips. But the photos didn't help much. I couldn't be sure that all of the starfish had been photographed in the same way, with the pin that attaches them to their wearer squarely horizontal across the back. Sometimes it seemed that the same stock photo was being used to announce the sale of any starfish, and I couldn't know if a piece had been pivoted for the most aesthetically attractive photo, which seemed likely. I asked Susan which two of her starfish's five rays were flipped at their ends, revealing a sliver of gold on their underside, like the hem of a flirty skirt. Perhaps the only way that the flipped rays on each piece could be evidence of which of the originals were being inspected was to have all three of them in front of me. That did not seem very likely to happen. Still, I kept a record of which rays were flipped. As a means of comparison, asking their owners to describe them this way worked, but I learned later that the two pins that attach the starfish are meant to be vertical in order to give it the best support.

I also asked Susan if her starfish was signed or bore a maker's mark. She put me on hold to go and get the brooch from her safe. When she returned she said that the engraving was small but she could make out "R. Boivin." There were some other marks, but nothing visible with the naked eye. No snake *poinçoin*, Boivin's hallmark. From her description I gathered that the second and fifth rays were the ones turned up at the end. She promised to send me a photo and we agreed to meet during my next trip to New York. She was intrigued by what further information I might have to share with her about the starfish. She did not know a lot about the starfish's history or the current interest in them. I asked her if she knew who its previous owner was. She paused to think. "I want to say Joanne Carson. A real estate person, I think," she said tentatively. Was Cummings the name? I asked. Yes, she corrected herself, she thought that was it. As soon as we hung up, I got out the Christie's auction records.

There is record of a starfish sale in April 1996 from the "Magnificent Jewels & Jewels from the Cummings Collection" at Christie's New York. I figured this must have been the starfish that Simon Teakle mentioned helping sell at Christie's that year. The text, in a typical example of the jewelry industry's lack of transparency, only reads, "The Property of A LADY." The description of the piece is the generic one that tells how sea life captured the imagination of Madame Boivin in 1936. Juliette Moutard, who joined Boivin in 1933, was the designer . . . Claudette Colbert had the first . . . I knew it now by heart. Françoise Cailles finished her description poetically by explaining, "Each arm was entirely articulated so that the jewel could reproduce the crawling movement of a living starfish." Well, not exactly. Despite this rather poetic claim, the starfish were more likely articulated so they could fit and conform to the place where the wearer chose to pin one. On a shoulder or bust or hat. Christie's added that "rubies and amethysts simulate the actual 'tube feet' and muscles that carry the creature on its way across the bottom of the sea." I can also see that while the projected sale price or value of the piece was estimated to be between $40,000 and $50,000, it sold for $79,500. Sadly, in the spot where the photo usually appears with the listing, there was a blank. "Image is not available," it read. Later, and after I had actually seen Susan's starfish for myself, I would see a photo of it in an old Christie's catalogue.

Neither were there more clues on Lotfinder, the search engine for auction sales, as to just what the Cummings Collection was. The auction house practice of naming sales for a collection that is included in an overall larger sale, even though other pieces of different provenance are added, made this more confusing. The title of the sale does not always suggest who owned the piece. I had previously asked Ward Landrigan about the name Cummings. "Nathan Cummings." He knew right away. "Mr. Sara Lee." That was how he had remembered who Nathan Cummings was. Jewelers, like art collectors, always know where the money comes from.

I remembered Sara Lee cakes, especially the frozen ones in the flat aluminum pans with banana cake and banana frosting. They'd been a treat in Richmond, Indiana. The company and Nathan Cummings had made a fortune.

Cummings died at age eighty-eight in 1985. He had amassed a huge art collection, including six hundred pieces of pre-Columbian art that would eventually go to the Metropolitan Museum of Art. Many of his fine pieces had at one time covered the walls of his ninth-floor apartment in the Waldorf Towers in New York City. Widowed from his first wife, Ruth Kellert, he married Joanne Toor, thirty-two years his junior, in 1959. They divorced in 1976.

During their marriage, the lively Joanne helped amass a collection of art, furniture, and fine jewelry. It is noteworthy, as I would soon learn was true of almost all the women who owned Boivin starfish, that she as a person was about more than baubles and bangles. Joanne had a master's degree from Columbia University's School of International Relations. Besides the philanthropy that she and Cummings sponsored, she had been a member of the National Committee of American Foreign Policy for nineteen years and its president for five. She wore designer clothes and beautiful jewelry, and when her estate was auctioned after her death, Christie's published a catalogue entitled "Jewels from the Collection of the Late Joanne Toor Cummings." The starfish was among them.

Despite writing to the Cummings Foundation and Joanne's sister Suzanne Tarpas in New York, I could never find out how Joanne Cummings acquired the starfish. No one who had known her personally was alive to tell me. It was well known that Nathan had started buying fine art in Paris in 1945. But at that time he was married to his first wife, Ruth. Their daughter, who lives in Chicago, inherited her mother's jewelry, but it did not include a starfish. Her best guess is that her father bought the starfish for Joanne. Nathan was also friends with the Duke and Duchess of Windsor, and the duchess was a well-known jewelry collector.

It was nearly six months before Susan Rotenstreich and I managed to meet for tea in New York. She arrived by chauffeured car at our appointed East Side location, and she was as pert and petite as the woman I had seen in photos online standing next to her tall husband in which the top of her head barely reaches his shoulder. She was an East Side version of Dolly Parton without the chest, I kept thinking. That may not do her justice. Her girlish energy, though she must have been nearly sixty, made her instantly likable. We thought we might have recognized each other from serving on the parent safety patrol at our children's high school. She was dressed smartly in tailored gray slacks that had a pearly sheen and a gray jacket. As we made small talk she told me that she was originally from Alabama, and that Southern-style warmth still shone through her sophisticated New Yorker patina. As I settled myself with a pad and paper to make notes she coyly took the starfish from her bag and placed it on the couch between us. She smiled at me playfully. "There it is." I was immediately taken aback by its size, but said nothing. I hoped I was concealing my disappointment. It was my second time encountering an actual starfish and I quickly picked it up, turned it over, and looked at its underside. This starfish was smaller and denser than the others, maybe fewer than four inches across. The original I had seen was almost five. Its impression was more compact, chubbier and tighter, than the one at Verdura, though its rays were beautifully articulated. Its movement was like a well-oiled piece of suit armor or an armadillo, as I imagined them. "Encrusted" was the word that came to mind. I counted the cabochon rubies that ran down the tops of its five rays. There were only five, not six, as I have counted and seen in the photos of those that have moved through Christie's since 1996 and been seen at Stephen Russell. Some of those, it is possible, were the same one being resold, but all of them were of the bigger design. Susan and I tried with our naked eyes to read the maker's mark on the underside. I have been told that two little engraved eagle eyes is the symbol that indicates eighteen-karat gold and sometimes the fabricator also had an engraved mark, but we could not make them out. "I don't really wear it that much," said Susan, a little apologetically, but it was clear that she admired it. I snapped a photo with my cell phone and this time savored its weight in my hand. Its relative small size confused me, but there was no reason to doubt its authenticity with the Boivin signage (I know, there remains that catch-22 about Boivin not signing them . . .) and the documentation from Christie's that accompanied its sale at auction. I thought the size might be an anomaly that I would just have to come to terms with, but I resolved to ask Françoise Cailles about it. I remembered that Jeanne Boivin liked to vary her designs slightly. There were two versions of her mermaid clip and several of a black-enameled gold ram. These variations, perhaps added by the designer both for creative fun and to help identify the pieces, definitely added fun and confusion for the chronicler—me.

Having accomplished our mission of looking at the starfish together, Susan and I made small talk for a few minutes while we finished our tea. She had already told me how she got it and how she wore it. Now Susan told me that she had embarked on a new profession, that of a licensed therapeutic touch practitioner, a modern-day healer who works with nurses and doctors to aid and hasten patients' recovery. Years ago I did a story on the nurse who pioneered the field, so I knew what she was talking about. "I love it. I've found my calling," she said, busting every preconceived notion I could have harbored about a wealthy New York woman who attends charity balls and has a collection of fine jewelry at her disposal. It would turn out that every woman I met who had a Boivin starfish was some sort of professional, fulfilling the premise that I had heard from dealers repeatedly that Boivin starfish attract a special clientele, a sophisticated thinking woman and not just a pampered rich pet. Imelda Marcos never had one. Not that I know of.

The size of Susan's starfish threw me for a bit of a loop. It was lovely, but it just didn't look like the photos in Cailles's book on Boivin or any of the other publications that featured Boivin's starfish. Yet it had come from Christie's with all the proper documentation. I couldn't know if perhaps Claudette Colbert's long-lost version had been smaller. Or if a smaller one had been made after Millicent Rogers's. I would have to wait to see another one to reach an informed conclusion. I sent a photo of it to Françoise Cailles and asked her opinion. There was no reply.

I had located one. There were three to go.

Chapter Eleven

WAS MAKING PROGRESS, I THOUGHT, AND THEN I HAD confirmation that the first brooch made by Boivin, the inspiration for how many others that followed, had been lost! Well—lost or stolen, or something. Claudette Colbert, its owner, seemed to have never been quite sure. Was it gone forever, or was it still out in that layered world of dealers and auctions somewhere, passing under a different identity? This was only going to complicate my search, and my attempts to sort out the brooches.

The prevailing opinion in the jewelry business, including jewelry books and auction houses, was that Boivin had made three original ruby and amethyst starfish brooches. Russell Zelenetz at Stephen Russell suggested there were four, and by adding two that were produced in the 1960s and 1980s, "later" versions, there might be even five or six, but it was the original three made and

sold by Boivin in Paris in the 1930s that interested me. Claudette
Colbert had owned the first one. Millicent Rogers had bought
the second. Her daughter-in-law had recently sold it and after it
showed up at my party, it had eventually been bought by Lee
Siegelson, who sold it to an unidentified (to me) buyer in New
York. The third was hard to pin down. As far as I could learn, it
had never appeared in public. I was running across hints that the
House of Boivin had not sold it, but held on and let its value increase. Then there were those pesky other two, rumored to have
been made later by Murray Mondschein, perhaps along with
others. I kept my hunt narrowed to learning the whereabouts of
the three originals.

The Hollywood actress Claudette Colbert came by her appreciation of French style and fashion quite naturally. Her baker father
brought his family to the United States from France when she was
only three, but an appreciation for things French stayed with her.
Blessed with good looks (her legs were legendary) and dramatic
talent, Claudette had the drive to succeed in the acting business.
She was an American success story in a time when most of them
were about men. Like Katharine Hepburn, Joan Crawford, and
other female movie stars in the thirties and forties, Claudette
seemed to understand the business, and she asserted control over
her career and finances early. She easily projected a persona of
glamour for her public, but behind the scenes she was known for
her perfectionism and an unyielding work ethic. Her trim and up-
right comportment had a touch of French hauteur. It seems fitting that she would have bought for herself the first Boivin ruby
and amethyst starfish brooch. Both she and her purchase were unapologetically bold, outsized beauties, just the kind of match that
designers hope to make for their creations.

Colbert had achieved movie star status in 1935 at age thirty-
one when she won an Oscar for her role in *It Happened One Night*,

a comedic caper, opposite Clark Gable. In it she played the spoiled
daughter of a Wall Street tycoon who deserted her blue-blooded
fiancé for a lowly newspaper reporter, played by Clark Gable. She
was the highest paid woman in Hollywood and was soon one of
the two highest paid *people* in Hollywood. (Movie mogul Jack War-
ner was the second.) To her admiring public she was known not
simply for her legs and knockout figure, but for an impeccable demeanor and dressing. Hers was a grown-up womanly glamour
that exuded taste and intelligent wit. Because of a bump—a slight
imperfection—on the right side of her nose, she would only al-
low herself to be photographed from the left. She popularized
Peter Pan collars because she knew that they helped to elongate
the appearance of her own short neck. Petite and compact at 108
pounds her entire life, she knew what made her look good and
demanded it in her pictures. Onscreen she wore figure-hugging,
showstopping finery that fed the imagination and luxurious fantasies of her Depression-weary audiences. Offscreen she took refuge
in Travis Banton's timeless, classic Eurochic suits and dresses. The
Texas-born Travis was the leading wardrobe designer for Para-
mount Pictures and had also been a favorite of silent-screen star
Mary Pickford. Claudette shared his smart, ladylike design sensi-
bility. She also loved jewelry. By this time, she could afford it.
Shrewdly, she had negotiated the colossal sum of fifty thousand
dollars, twice her usual shooting salary and five times Clark Gable's
take for their Oscar-winning movie, when she visited the Boivin
salon in search of an electrifying piece of jewelry.

Colbert and her two husbands had no children, but she was nonetheless a woman who observed family ties and loyalites. When
separated from her first husband, she lived with her mother for
seven years, and she stayed connected with her niece, Coco Lewis,
throughout her life. Lewis, a Realtor in Fremont, California, told
me that an appreciation for jewelry ran in the family. Her father,

Claudette's brother, admired jewelry enough to lavish it on his six wives, including her mother. Lewis grew up appreciating quality pieces and knew that Claudette had a fine collection, including a brooch by Tiffany that she saw later in a public exhibit. But she says she never saw the starfish.

In Claudette Colbert's later life, when her acting career had cooled and she was widowed by her second husband, she moved at the center of an energetic private life that increasingly came to rely on a woman twenty-seven years her junior, Helen O'Hagan. O'Hagan, single and also childless, had been a marketing executive at Saks Fifth Avenue and worked with designers who created some of Colbert's clothes on- and off-screen. Claudette befriended O'Hagan and took her under her wing. Colbert, it was well known among her close friends like socialite Leonora Hornblow and Nancy Reagan, did not like being alone. She was an actress to the core and needed, if not an audience, at least a listener. Whether it was her long-term maid Marie Corbin from Barbados, or Helen, she wanted someone to live with her and thought nothing of waking them at night when she came in if she simply wanted to recap her evening or talk. O'Hagan was invited to move into Claudette's last Fifth Avenue apartment and learned about her, her habits, and her jewelry collection. I hoped that Helen O'Hagan, who had then outlived Colbert by almost twenty years, would know about Claudette's starfish.

It was a somewhat clouded story.

Since Claudette's death in 1996, O'Hagan has been the keeper of her flame. Helen blends into the army of trim-trousered and well-heeled women of a certain age on Manhattan's East Side. Behind her big red-framed glasses, she listened attentively to me outline my quest. She seemed to be trying to place the starfish.

She was executor of Claudette's $3.5 million estate and also largely her heir, a role that Claudette's community of friends and distant family did not begrudge her, since she had pretty single-handedly taken care of the aging actress following a stroke the last six years of her life. Helen says that it was she who had a safe built into their apartment for Claudette's valuables. Until then, Claudette had preferred keeping her jewelry collection in the safe-deposit box at the Chase bank branch on the corner nearby her Fifth Avenue apartment. There was also a safe in the actress's Barbados home, a two-hundred-acre plantation estate where she spent most of her time during her later years. In New York, when Claudette planned to go out wearing a piece of her fine jewelry, she sent their maid, Marie, to get it out of her safe-deposit box and carry it home. She was also known for being careless, misplacing pieces or losing track of them. So Helen suggested the safe.

O'Hagan continues to live in the coral-walled apartment that looks down into Central Park. It is kept as something of a shrine to Claudette with newspaper clippings about the actress in open stationery boxes and unfinished scrapbooks scattered around. Unhung artwork stood against the walls, but Claudette's Oscar has its perch on a corner cabinet shelf. Filled with its pinks and chintzes, the apartment feels wholly feminine, cluttered, and just beginning to slip out of its resident's control. When I visited, Helen was gracious and charming.

She explained Claudette's insouciance toward her belongings of value. "She didn't designate where anything should go when she died," O'Hagan said, and while some cash went to her maid of forty years, Marie, Helen says that she auctioned Claudette's personal items of value, like jewelry, through Christie's auction house in California after her death. She seemed genuinely intrigued by my quest and promised to look determinedly through some of her boxes of photographs to see if Claudette was ever photographed with the starfish. She also referred me to several close friends and neighbors of Claudette's who might have seen her wear it.

Without seeming to recognize or remember a ruby and amethyst starfish brooch, Helen made several guesses as to what happened to it. Claudette, it seems, was so famously careless with her jewelry that she often impulsively gave a piece away, Helen explained. A persistent note of kindness and generosity runs through most accounts of Claudette's relationships. Still, it was difficult to imagine that she would have given away the starfish. Claudette was quite astute about the value of things and auctioneers had mentioned that she had sometimes removed the stones from settings that she put up for sale. But perhaps anything is possible with rich women and jewelry.

There had been thefts. As Helen racked her brain to remember incidents of theft or loss during the years she spent with Claudette, she ran over certain possibilities. There had been a robbery of Claudette's room in Rome during a trip to visit Wanda Ferragamo of the shoemaking dynasty. Helen had been traveling with her and stayed in the room across the hall when jewelry that Claudette had left out disappeared while she was sleeping. Helen says it was assumed that someone had entered through a door that opened to the balcony. The same memory led her to recall that Claudette had been friendly with the composer Cole Porter. He and his wife Linda Lee were well-known jewelry collectors and aficionados, especially of Verdura. Linda commissioned a jeweled cigarette case for each of her husband's musicals that opened on Broadway. Helen thinks it likely that the Porters introduced Claudette to Boivin in the 1930s, which would explain how she made her way to the salon on the Avenue de l'Opéra and purchased the brooch in the first place. But the details of the starfish's disappearance from her life are less certain.

Her best guess is that Claudette lost the piece with a bag of jewelry in the 1950s in Paris. "It was in the airport or train station," Helen recalled being told. Her relationship with Claudette began several decades later, but Claudette had talked about losing the bag and its contents. Helen rambled back to the story she had heard. It was a blue Pan American carry-on bag, a staple of fashionable transatlantic travelers in the fifties and sixties, that Claudette had left on a seat in a waiting room or train station.

By this point in my search for the starfish I had learned that it is not unusual for heirs or housekeepers to spirit away valuable pieces of jewelry that disappear from public sight. But Helen just didn't seem the type. There was no reason to believe she was someone who would steal from her mistress. Claudette had cared and provided for her almost like a daughter, and I believed her story. The starfish didn't seem to register with Helen when I showed her a photo of it. She didn't remember it. If she was faking, she was an actress to rival Claudette. However, if the starfish had been lost or given away before they met, she could not have seen it. She did remember some pieces of Claudette's jewelry, like a diamond pin that Claudette's friend, the collector of Asian art Bob Ellsworth, bought when it came up for sale at auction after the actress's death. Helen simply didn't seem to know about the starfish. She only remembered that Claudette sometimes mourned the jewelry that she had lost in that Pan Am bag. With her penchant for drama, the actress had wrung her hands over her foolishness and blamed herself for the loss, but she didn't itemize its contents during her lament. And Helen's account, recited to me several times over a year or so, varied slightly. Sometimes the bag was left in the Paris train station, sometimes the airport. It seemed clear that she was trying to help, but she just didn't know.

Few of Claudette's coterie of close friends are alive today, but two former neighbors and associates, Bob and Helen Bernstein, still live in New York. The Bernsteins are parents of a friend and contemporary of mine, Peter Bernstein, who put me in touch with them. They seemed slightly amused that I was investigating an old piece of Claudette's jewelry. Helen Bernstein recalled little beyond Claudette's understated taste in clothes and that she maintained her fabulous figure. During those days, the late fifties and sixties, Claudette is remembered for smart but plain dressing and certainly not for any ostentatious jewelry, a category that certainly includes Boivin starfish. Neither Bernstein ever saw her wear a ruby and amethyst starfish brooch.

The other friend in this triumvirate of neighbors on East Sixty-fourth Street who had known Claudette Colbert was Bob Ellsworth, a legendary collector of Asian art in New York. He once had a gallery on East Fifty-sixth Street, and when Claudette traveled between Hollywood and Barbados she often stayed with him before she purchased her own apartment or when it was rented out.

It was freezing cold the day I went to see Robert Hatfield Ellsworth in his wonderfully elegant twenty-room Fifth Avenue apartment in New York. His staff and caretaker had told me he was in fragile health and I was expecting to find a much frailer eighty-eight-year-old man than the one who awaited me when his son ushered me into his study. Ellsworth was wearing a leather vest and a gold-striped shirt with cuff links when he rose to meet me. His impeccably appointed drawing room was brightly lit through five draped windows, two looking into Central Park below. Buddhas, Japanese paintings, and other South Asian artifacts were displayed on the mantel of the fireplace and throughout the room. I was heartened that this man, considered among the biggest collectors of Asian art in the world, and clearly an aesthete, might remember his friend Claudette's jewelry. I walked across a beautiful rug with a dragon motif woven into its pastel center in front of a glowing fire in the fireplace to sit across from him at his green morocco leather-topped desk by the window. A brass statue of a griffon held a small supply of silk-cut cigarettes. He lit one.

I noticed that several framed photos in the room contained photographs of Claudette. He had met Claudette, he said, when he worked as an appraiser of Chinese antiques and Claudette was his neighbor on East Sixty-fourth, the same building where the Bernsteins had stayed. His account of her was the same as I had heard before. She was charming, natural, a wonderful friend, and always a lady. When I showed him a life-sized photograph of the ruby and amethyst starfish, he paused for a second and took it in. "I would have thrown it in the fireplace," if he'd seen it, he said dismissively. It was too big and gaudy for him. And that was the end of that.

I had to accept that Claudette's starfish brooch, like its prototype that lives under the sea, had silently slipped out of sight.

Yet Bob Bernstein had given me an insight into Claudette. She had an indulgent nature. Claudette did not live entirely in Peter Pan collars sporting small pieces of jewelry. She could be extravagant, a detail that Bob learned from Claudette's husband Jack, when Claudette had rented a house in the south of France one summer. Bob Bernstein, on the thrifty side, asked why Claudette needed that house when she already had places in Barbados and New York. "Bob," explained Jack good-naturedly. "You obviously have no experience with movie stars. Claudette wants to buy shoes in Paris. If she has a house in the south of France she can go to Paris for shoes."

Claudette was clearly a woman with the moxie and money to buy herself a ruby and amethyst starfish brooch the size of her hand for no greater reason than liking it. She did not have to account for herself to anyone. I could imagine Claudette, her fabulous legs crossed at the ankles, sitting with perfect posture, perhaps wearing the toffee-colored Travis Banton skirt suit and lush brown mink coat she had worn at the Biltmore Hotel in Los Angeles on Oscar night, poised before Jeanne Boivin at the sweeping counter in the shimmering Paris salon and deciding, with her newfound fame and at the peak of her power, to buy the starfish. It must have been a marvelous high. What is harder to understand is how no one remembers her wearing it, selling it, or owning it. Yet its original purchase by her is recounted in nearly every sale of the brooch since and is widely accepted as fact.

When Claudette bought her ruby and amethyst starfish brooch it was unusual for women to buy their own jewelry. Few made enough money on their own to purchase such an extravagant piece. Jewelry was invariably a gift given to women by men, yet another reason for so much secrecy in the business. Men often gave jewelry to women besides their wives, a point that Ward Landrigan at Verdura pointed out to me when he explained why most jewelry houses had two entrances in case a wife and a mistress happened to be there at the same time, God forbid, one with the husband. At least one party could escape unobserved. For a rich man with a formal mistress, jewelry was a commodity and a way to transfer wealth unnoticed.

It took a certain degree of confidence and determination to bring off wearing a Boivin starfish. But Claudette Colbert and the glamorous heiress Millicent Rogers, who bought the second, had a bounty of both. Both made their own fashion rules and statements. Before 1930 appropriate jewelry for women had been rather tightly dictated by fashion convention. There were lots of guidelines. Small pieces dominated, especially as American culture experienced the Great Depression. Lavish jewels were worn onscreen in Hollywood to give audiences a lift and a vicarious thrill, but offscreen, dainty and discreet were the prevailing principles governing jewelry fashion for women. Costume jewelry had not come into vogue yet. However, the starfish and a few other pieces that were coming out of Paris at the time began to point jewelry trends for fashionable, rich women in a different direction. Coco Chanel, in league with Fulco di Verdura, was sporting big Maltese cuff bracelets. Other trendsetters, such as Mona Bismarck, Mrs. Harrison Williams, and wealthy women on the best-dressed lists of the day, were wearing big rings, bracelets, necklaces, and brooches and buying them for themselves. The movie star Joan Crawford bought herself a diamond and platinum bracelet. These women were like American princesses and typically bought their own fine jewelry, a practice that would be copied in the 1970s by working women when they altered the dynamic by buying their own, less extravagant pieces.

By the 1930s, word among the stylish international set was, "Everyone goes to Belperron or Boivin." Daisy Fellowes, Josephine Baker, and Lady Diana Cooper were already clients. When Claudette walked in she was looking for something special. Her everyday look was generally a strand of pearls at her throat and diamond earrings, but she wanted something different. Something bold. Helen O'Hagan can imagine the appeal of the starfish because Claudette was partial always to maritime motifs. Even in her house in Barbardos, some years later, she had starfish sink faucets and dolphin fixtures on the tub.

In the mid-thirties, articulated pieces were also catching on, if not the rage. Belperron had created butterflies with wings that could move on hinges. Her designs in the late twenties, while she was still working at Boivin, were hailed as "bold and barbaric" by *Vogue*. By 1933 the fashion magazine's editors wrote of the revival of "big jewels," and by 1934 sea motifs, shells, and other creatures were cropping up in the pages of *Harper's Bazaar* (March 1934) and *Vogue*. This drift to finely articulated naturalism wasn't wholly due to whims of taste and style, but also to metallurgy, especially the appearance of platinum, which gave jewelers a metal with more strength to work with. Of course, the starfish are eighteen-karat yellow gold and the pairing of yellow gold with colored stones was based on trend as much as practicality. Goldsmithing was being constantly refined. Working with real gold allowed pieces to be crafted by hand without the excess involved in using the lost-wax casting method that would take hold in the 1950s. Fabricators discussed their progress with designers sometimes daily, eliminating missteps and extra costs. Boivin tapped thirty workers in Paris who were considered the best in the city and the best paid.

Stone setting and polishing had also evolved. Diana Vreeland, Elsa Schiaparelli, and the trendsetting Daisy Fellowes, heiress to the Singer sewing machine empire, all had Boivin pieces by 1938. They were massive and personal. "If you have but one jewel, do have a colossal one," trumpeted *Vogue* in its July 15 issue in 1933. The starfish could only have been a purchase for a buyer of means, yet it appeared as an "it" accessory in a 1937 edition of *Vogue*. "René Boivin turns out a bit of realism in ruby-studded gold. He made the star-shaped clip amazingly lifelike and flexible so that it moves rather appallingly when it's touched," wrote *Harper's Bazaar* ten months later.

In some ways Millicent's jewelry tastes and the shopping habits that pointed her to the Boivin salon mirrored Claudette Colbert's in the 1930s. These were independent-minded, glamorous women with the money to indulge themselves and liked jewelry to mirror their verve and good looks. I hoped that the path of Millicent's starfish out of Paris would be easier to follow than Colbert's seeming dead end. It was also a puzzle to me how various versions—subtly different—of such a wonderful design were produced in that magical French atelier, acquired by glamorous buyers, and then scattered or disappeared, their uniqueness to be undermined by copies. Colbert's had mysteriously vanished, and what had become of the third? I had to seek people who knew the game, but were not, at least to my knowledge, current players.

Chapter Twelve

FRENCH JEWELRY DESIGN HISTORY AND BUSINESS practices have evolved ever since Napoleon I determined to make France the epicenter of luxury goods and style for the Western world. I sought out a reputable, seasoned French jeweler in New York to help me understand. André Chervin of Carvin French Jewelers on Madison Avenue, I hoped, would sort out questions about the conditions under which Boivin would have made several copies of the same piece, the landmark starfish brooch.

In his unembellished office behind a series of white security doors, Chervin, unpretentious in a short-sleeved dress shirt, strove to be as generous and helpful as possible to me in my quest to understand Boivin. He had been in the jewelry business for seventy years, he told me with an amused twinkle and a smile.

He asked me about my story and the progress I had made so far. "People in the jewelry business can be petty, I think," he said in his soft French accent when he heard that some jewelers were reluctant to discuss the pieces. He was dubious that people tell the truth. "These are not state secrets. They are industry secrets," he said, gently mocking the attitudes of the jewelry trade. He once had a Boivin ruby and amethyst starfish in his salon that was brought to him for repair but he says he could not accept it. "It was too . . . Perhaps it had been dropped." He shrugged, but he remembered its striking beauty. People always remember its beauty.

I wanted to know what conventions or rules governed the making of copies of the starfish. It was a topic that would occupy more of my thought and reporting on the starfish than I knew at the time. Chervin guessed that the drawing of the first starfish was never shown to Colbert, but that Moutard and Jeanne Boivin simply decided to make one. Then after it turned out to be spectacular and was bought by Colbert, they hoped to make another. "Ah, but there is always the question of privacy. It is like spending a lot of money for a dress. You don't want to see another!" he said. Jeanne Boivin well understood the need for women to feel that the piece of jewelry they purchased from her was unique. Later the Parisian jeweler Emmanuelle Chassard showed me a Boivin ram at a jewelry show in Miami that looked straight ahead in the version she had for sale, but in a photo of the piece in Boivin's catalogue its head of curled horns was turned to the side. Small variations could make enough difference to make a design noticeably unique, but allowed a favorite to be fabricated several times. I wondered if Susan Rotenstreich's smaller version was an example of this practice.

According to French law, Chervin explained, a jeweler was licensed to make three models of an original design at once. Overproducing would have diluted the value of the piece in an era before mass production was common, and the French carefully regulated their arts. Chervin guessed that the first starfish had been already made when it was sold to Colbert and that she did not order it from a drawing. He thinks that Moutard and Boivin were most likely smitten enough by the design to make it without having a buyer in the wings. After it turned out to be a stunning piece and was sold to an American movie star, they would have hoped to create another. When Rogers, already a regular client, came in to see what was new at the Boivin salon in the Palais-Royal, *voilà!* They had something special to show her.

There could have been a starfish sitting in the long sweeping jewelry case when Millicent swooped in with her usual charm and hauteur to shop. Or, as André Chervin explained, it is more likely that Madame Boivin, or perhaps even the legendary salesman and director of the showroom, Monsieur Girard, skillfully stoked her interest. "There is something you might like that we have made, but I will have to ask if I may show it to you," Chervin explained such careful salesmanship. This was the protocol if Colbert had commissioned hers, or maybe even as a courtesy if she had simply bought the first one already made. "Saying 'we made something but we cannot propose it to you without asking' would have gotten her attention," he explained, wise to the ways of creating interest in a piece of jewelry. I asked if Claudette Colbert would have cared. Chervin laughed one of those infectious French male laughs that makes you feel for a brief moment that you have said something original and clever when you know you have been neither. "I could care less is what she probably said," he rejoined. But in his opinion the jeweler would have played the role of being punctiliously discreet and would have also tickled Millicent's interest by creating an element of suspense and something to wait for. Of course, I thought as I left him, Millicent would have ordered one to her specifications. It is not surprising that her starfish differed slightly from the others.

Rogers and Colbert did not know each other, but I had heard from O'Hagan that Colbert admired Rogers's style and the influence she cast over fashion in their day—the thirties and forties. It is a somewhat ironic aside that their taste dovetailed in jewelry and men. After Rogers divorced Ronnie Balcom, he appeared in a photograph taken on the ski slopes in Sun Valley with Colbert at his side.

The other two original starfish that were created by Boivin in the 1930s were fully articulated, but Rogers's was not. Its rays have movable joints but they do not bend as fully as the others. This is hard to know if you don't handle the piece and have the benefit of comparing it to the others whose golden joints go slack if you dangle them in the air. But Millicent's starfish also had another key difference. Hers was the only starfish that had baguette amethysts circling the big round ruby at its center. The baguettes, or little rectangles, are the distinguishing feature I am most grateful for because they are the only way to know from a photo whether a starfish was Millicent's. They have been the best evidence that after my date with it that night at my book party at Verdura, I have not seen the Rogers starfish again.

Chapter Thirteen

MILLICENT ROGERS WAS ATTRACTED TO THE Boivin starfish for the same reasons it had captivated Claudette Colbert. She always had an eye for stylish jewelry, and liked to make a splash. Her father scolded her in a letter for overspending when she was in her twenties. By the time she was in her thirties and living in Europe, it was a full-blown avocation. Major jewelers like Boivin often saw her coming. They knew she had money to spend and seldom asked the price of something that she wanted, but there was a flip side to her shopping habits. She was a difficult client, full of the sense of entitlement that great wealth bestows. The Belperron archives made note of her attempts to return pieces sometimes years after she had bought them in hopes of exchanging them for newer designs. Rogers was determined to live on the stylish cusp of change, and most shoppers didn't act like her. With less money to spend, they didn't have her clout with merchants, who always forgave her excesses.

Millicent was an extravagant collector of jewelry and she learned to make pieces of her own design, both reasons that led her to Boivin in Paris in the 1930s. Boivin's imaginative and innovative styles had already captivated several Hollywood personalities in the United States. Couturiers like Millicent's friend Elsa Schiaparelli were acquainted with Boivin because they knew Jeanne's brother, Paul Poiret, the leading fashion designer in Paris before the war. Poiret was inspired by Serge Diaghilev's Ballets Russes to introduce flowing styles that were a precursor to flapper fashions in the United States. The dancer Isadora Duncan and the actress legend Sarah Bernhardt were also clients, and popularized Boivin's bold jewelry styles. Rogers was attracted to Boivin jewelry not only for the wonderful naturalistic designs that were becoming the rage, but she also found the ambience of a house run by women that also relied on women designers especially appealing as she tried to learn jewelry making for herself. She had sent one of her own early efforts at design to Boivin for fabrication. She was acquainted with Jeanne's brother, Paul Poiret. They traveled in the same well-connected fashion circles. It was a genial relationship that would lead Rogers, with her appetite for high-quality novelty in clothes and accessories, to come eventually across the Boivin starfish.

Remember, she *was* a Standard Oil heiress, and her appetite for collecting was insatiable. Jewelry occupied a central part of her life. Rogers had suffered from rheumatic fever as a child and she suffered throughout her life from a weak heart. A series of small strokes caused some paralysis and tremors in her left arm. Jewelry making, the wielding of small jewelers' tools and the shaping of wax models, was good for maintaining her manual dexterity. She also liked presenting personalized gifts, like the gold cuff links she made for Clark Gable.

As she did with dress couturiers, Rogers influenced designs with leading jewelers that she patronized. She was instrumental in Fulco di Verdura's creation of a diamond-thronged scallop-shell brooch and she contributed design motifs to the leading American jeweler Paul Flato. Her design, the Flato heart brooch, was the same one Lee Seigelson gave me to try on when I first met him and Sarah Davis in the Siegelson salon.

In 1938 Rogers married her third husband, the handsome bon vivant Ronnie Balcom, nine years her junior. They occupied a house that she and her second husband, an Argentine aristocrat, had built in Austria, and during the years they spent there before World War II, Millicent exemplified, as Diana Vreeland put it, *soignée* international fashion style. She shopped in Paris and wore designs by the leading couturiers of the day, including Valentina, Schiaparelli, and Mainbocher. In addition to modeling her style in *Harper's Bazaar* and *Vogue*, she often accessorized the clothes she wore for fashion shoots with her own pieces of jewelry. She showed up with the Flato heart brooch coming through customs with Ronnie Balcom and on a Schiaparelli suit that she modeled for *Vogue*. In the photo she sits at the desk of her New York apartment in a Schiaparelli black pantsuit with the starfish pinned to her right shoulder in 1945. Like Claudette Colbert, Millicent bought her starfish for herself in 1938.

That year she had given Ronnie, a car fancier, a Delage Aerosport coupe that he admired at the Paris Expo. The deal was contingent on the manufacturer's adopting a new shape she had specified for the fender and rear fin. Rogers never needed an excuse for parity in spending, but that gift is the closest I can come to a motivation for her buying a ruby and amethyst starfish brooch for herself, if she needed a justification. She rarely did. It is more probable that she was simply captivated by the starfish, prized it for its beauty, and bought it for herself. Because she had more money than the men she kept in her life, they did not buy jewelry for her. She bought her own.

Both the first two starfish were bought by wealthy, stylish women for themselves, which suggested a pattern that would continue. It also bore out the theory of some jewelers that the starfish attracted a unique kind of woman. The first shared attribute was being rich, but it went beyond money.

Like Colbert, Rogers had confidence and flair enough to sport a piece as bold as the starfish. This was a woman who had gone to a New York debutante's ball in a black dress and Chinese headdress for no better reason than to create a sensation. She almost always tweaked the design of things she bought, changing the buttons on coats, mixing rustic and refined elements in clothes, putting her personal stamp on everything she touched. So it is reasonable to assume that she did the same thing with the starfish that she had done in the Delage showroom where she had taken a lipstick out of her purse and drawn the tail fin design she wanted on the car she ordered for her husband. At Boivin, she likely asked Juliette Moutard and Jeanne Boivin to make her starfish a bit different from the one Claudette Colbert had. She wanted hers to be slightly more rigid and to lie flatter than the more articulated variety that Claudette had bought. Records show that she ordered the starfish and a hippocamp piece by Boivin at the same time. She was accustomed to asking for a slightly different, personalized twist to most things she had custom made. She was also known for her great tact with designers, making them feel that she was only suggesting the smallest modification to their own already brilliant creations. Juliette Moutard and Jeanne Boivin either demurred or concurred. It is worth noting that the next starfish Boivin would produce after Rogers's reverted to Juliette's original design, fully articulated again and without baguette amethysts around the central cabochon ruby. Perhaps Millicent's was even the third that was made, though it was the second that sold, if Jeanne Boivin had taken advantage of the French law to make two more of the first design. The evidence suggests that Jeanne and Juliette preferred their original design. As for the phantom third, I was still looking for even one report that someone had seen it outside of the shop.

The Rogers family, I hoped, would have the story of how Millicent's starfish had come up for sale in 2011. I took a deep breath. Millicent's last living son, Arturo Peralta Ramos, had not been the easiest source to deal with while I was writing his mother's biography. But I was hearing from diverse parties in the jewelry business who had anything to do with the selling of Millicent's starfish that Arturo had owned the piece, and to make the story even juicier, that he and his wife had at last opened up a safe where he kept it in his New York apartment, formerly his mother's, along with other treasured and valuable pieces of jewelry. I had perked up when Claudine Seroussi, as part of our early conversation about the Rogers piece, told me the story of a young couple she had met who announced themselves to be Rogers family of some sort and spoke of a storied safe.

Rogers had grandchildren, but none came to mind that fit this description, and the idea of a vault where Millicent's remaining gems were hidden sounded to me like something right out of Arturo's storybook. He loved intrigue and secrets. But I listened. I also heard that Arturo and his wife Jackie, who previously spent summers in Turtlewalk, the old hacienda in Taos that Millicent had bought and refurbished in the 1940s, were now living in Taos full-time. Arturo was eighty-seven and in spite of smoking several packs of cigarettes a day he managed to carry on, driving around an old woody station wagon with the tanks of oxygen he needed to keep breathing at an altitude of seven thousand feet in the seat next to him.

I had heard that Jackie, also in her eighties, had been the actual owner of the starfish until it was sold. I made an appointment to speak with her but she insisted that I talk to Arturo first since he had known about the starfish longer than she had.

A pack of barking dogs announced my arrival at the house. Arturo met me at the top of the outdoor stairs to his study and ushered me inside, ready to talk about his mother's starfish brooch.

Arturo guessed that his mother found her way to Boivin with "Schiap," her designer and friend Elsa Schiaparelli. "Schiap introduced her to jewelers. My mother had tons and tons of jewelery," he said, and added that she carried it with her during their trips to Paris, where she often stayed at the Plaza Athénée. These memories swam around for Arturo. He recalled a ring from the 1920s that had belonged to the Russian mystic Rasputin in his mother's collection. Its connection to a villainous and powerful figure captured his boyish imagination. "She would pay any price if she wanted it," he said of his mother's shopping method. Millicent seemed to have few true favorite pieces of jewelry, he recalled, but "she wore the starfish on gowns. I remember that." He spoke knowingly of Millicent's visits to Boivin though he could not remember there being a specific time or day that she came home to Shulla House in Austria with a jewelry purchase from Paris, where she often traveled to visit her mother when the family lived in Europe before World War II. He did remember the starfish being in their house and seeing his mother wear it. He told me that Millicent followed a quote from "Johnny" (Jean) Schlumberger, who designed for Tiffany & Co.: "If you can't wear it, why have it?" She wore her jewelry.

The most provocative new thing Arturo told me about the starfish was his teenage memory of Millicent having two of them. He said that he remembered the starfish because when he saw two of them, he asked her, "Why do you want a second one?" She answered that she was "comparing" them. Stylish women and men to whom I have posed the same question have said that two would have made a fabulous belt buckle. Arturo always remembered having the impression that the second starfish had arrived for Millicent to take a look at and somehow to evaluate or appraise. Whatever the reason, she only kept one for her collection. On occasion she loaned it to friends to wear—or to study. Arturo remembered it being loaned to his grandmother Mary and to the Hollywood actress Janet Gaynor. He thought it may have also been loaned to the Brazilian sculptress Maria Martens, who encouraged Millicent to have confidence in her own jewelry-making talent and designs.

After Millicent died in 1952 her will left certain pieces like her pearl ring and earrings to family members, but Arturo seems to have kept what jewelry was not itemized in her will. He says that after he married his second wife, Jackie, he started giving her a "pin" from his mother's collection every year at Christmas. The first one he gave to her was the starfish.

Discussing the starfish gave Arturo reason to tell me a touching story that I had heard before but not in such detail. His mother had met his second-wife-to-be when she was just a teenager in the San Fernando Valley. Millicent was in her forties and had moved to Los Angeles to be closer to her new lover, Clark Gable. She was looking at property to buy, inspecting the movie director John Ford's farm, not far from his existing home in Encino, California, where the thirteen-year-old Jackie rode her horse. Jackie was upset at seeing the surveyor's sticks on the land where she loved to ride and considered wild, so on three occasions she jumped down from her horse on her daily ride and pulled them up, thinking she could impede any sale of the property. Finally, the third time, Gable and Millicent caught her doing it. According to Arturo, Gable scolded her roughly, threatening to spank her for what she had done "to this lady." Millicent took a gentler line with

Jackie, who explained that she had meant no harm. She simply wanted to be able to ride her horse on the property. "Come and ride here anytime," Millicent assured her. And Jackie rode home chastened but sure that "the lady," Millicent, loved horses because of a large pin she was wearing on her shirt. In fact, the pin was Boivin's famous hippocamp brooch, startling for its image of a half horse, half merhorse: a "hippocamp" dangling a dark gray drop-shaped pearl. The hippocamp would reenter her life again later.

I went to visit Jackie a few days after I had spoken with Arturo. Jackie was a former couture model easing into her eighties. She was still remarkably attractive. I knew that she had been plagued in recent years by health issues and I expected someone more frail, ravaged even, than the immaculately dressed, creamy-skinned, slender woman who greeted me. The housekeeper ushered me down a hallway lined with blue oxygen tubes to her bedroom. She suffered from emphysema but she was breathing without oxygen when I arrived. There was an element of animated fun about her that is hard to describe, as though she just might jump out of bed and dance the twist or share a secret with you. And she was elegant in chartreuse and black lounging pajamas, her silky blond-white hair pulled back with a headband à la fifties Hollywood. Her nails were neatly manicured and polished to a neutral sheen. Her bedroom at Turtlewalk looked north across the fields of Taos. Majestic Taos Mountain appeared through the large picture window framed with tasseled drapes. Between the foot of her bed and the window a large flat-screen television was on, tuned to horseracing, one of her passions. I asked if we could lower the volume while I sat at the foot of the bed as she talked about her starfish.

She said Arturo had given the starfish brooch to her for

their first wedding anniversary. "I opened the box and it was the pin. 'Where'd you get this?'" she recalled asking gleefully. Her voice still had a girlish bounce to it. "He told me it was his mother's."

She had kept it in the vault of their New York apartment that had also been his mother's. "I loved the starfish. My daughter didn't like it and Paullie didn't like it," she said, referring to her stepdaughter, Lorian, and Arturo's younger brother, Paul. She lit up when recounting the occasions when she wore it. "I walked into À La Vieille Russie with it. I was wearing a beige tweed suit with the pin. I loved it," she enthused. She recalled wearing it one night on a cruise ship. Cole Porter, who was with his wife, Linda, asked, "Is that real?" One can hear her charming them, her lilting voice explaining that of course it was real.

She figures that she wore it two or three dozen times in the forty-seven years that she had it, but she said there are downsides to owning jewelry of its kind, big and highly valued. "You can be robbed or hit on the head," she said, laughing a little, and I understood why so many people I had met in Taos liked Jackie and had remembered having good times in her company. "But you can't wear jewelry like it much anymore. It is too big. There is no denying what it is. That's why it sat in the vault for years and years." Ever since the day when she rode her horse through property that Clark Gable and Millicent Rogers were interested in buying, Jackie has been a horse fancier. She owned a dozen racehorses and said that it was a string of losses at the track that forced her to sell the starfish. "I needed the money for stud fees. Racehorses are so expensive! The boarding and training." She rolled her eyes sheepishly, admitting her folly. A stud fee can run $65,000, she complained.

"I was never a jewelry lover, to tell you the truth," she observed, explaining her frankness in confessing that she had few qualms about parting with pieces in general, but as for the starfish, she said, "I loved it. It was the last thing I let go."

Abruptly, she asked if I would object to her having a cigarette and then quickly asked me not to tell Arturo that she was smoking. I tried to keep a straight face since the house already smelled of smoke and I doubted Arturo would know the difference. She suddenly procured a pack of Misty, slender, thin menthols. It may have been my question about who she sold the starfish to and why that made her want a cigarette. "He was the biggest crook!" she said, her eyes sharp and alert from a jolt of adrenaline or the nicotine. "I feel so stupid!" The "he" she was referring to, she explained, was Henry Baker.

This was a name I had heard before from Lee Siegelson. When I first asked Lee, before I was into the starfish's saga with both feet, how he had acquired the Rogers starfish, he quickly ran through the story for me. "A guy" who worked for another jeweler, Oscar Heyman, on Madison Avenue, near Siegelson at 589 Fifth Avenue, made the rounds with the starfish to show to jewelers. Who was this guy? I asked. His name was Henry Baker and he worked for Heyman, one of the finest manufacturers of fine jewelry in the United States today. Lee said he had sold a starfish in the 1990s and Henry Baker probably knew that. I wondered how such a person carried the starfish to shop it around. "He just brought it in in his pocket. It's no big deal," Lee explained. He would soon, I learned later, pay three hundred thousand dollars for the starfish to a London dealer who had backed Henry Baker's purchase of it.

Listening to Jackie, I flashed back to my first visit with Siegelson, when he was looking for the granddaughter who had been instrumental in the sale of Jackie's starfish. I had never spoken to her, but Jackie was now filling in the blanks.

Her stepdaughter, Lorian Buckley, Arturo's daughter from his first marriage, is an art historian who has friends in the jewelry business in Connecticut. When she heard that Jackie wanted to sell some of her jewelry to cover expenses for her horses, Lorian made the connection with an old friend who dabbled in jewelry and was also a friend of Henry Baker's.

Numbers are not things that any of these people, sellers, dealers, or buyers want to talk about, but I gathered that about $140,000 was paid for three pieces of jewelry that Henry purchased out of the Ramos's safe. They were the starfish, the hippocamp that the teenaged Jackie had seen Millicent Rogers wearing when she was caught pulling up the surveyor's stakes in Encino, and a starburst pin. Their sales would later tally more than a million dollars. Jackie fumed over the thought that Henry had made a killing. "Oh, someone comes and sits and talks to you and you buy their phoniness and the lies," she said, knocking the horse magazine near her feet off the bed. "I loved it and it was the last thing I let go. I am so ashamed," she said. But she quickly justified the sale, explaining that she did it for her horses. "They are my children!"

Buckley shared her own magical memory of the starfish. When she was eight years old it belonged to her mother, Dusty, Arturo's first wife. "I remember Mother's dressing table and that there was this thing sitting on a red leather jewelry box and seeing that it was bigger than my hand and the most amazing thing to look at. I'll remember it for a hundred years!" she said excitedly. "It and the hippocamp," she said, referring to the half-horse, half-sea-monster creation, also by Juliette Moutard. Millicent's hippocamp was a golden seahorse in an emerald-lined scallop shell serving as Poseidon's chariot. A saltwater pearl dangled from a ruby bow. In fact, the history of the hippocamp, perhaps inspired by the mythical sea creatures in the Trevi fountain, is more complex and fantastic than the starfish, but it is a hard piece of jewelry to like, let alone wear. If it is difficult for contemporary women, even some of the present-day owners like Susan Rotenstreich, to wear the starfish because of its size and the large statement it makes, try pinning the hippocamp to a lapel. (Of course, Millicent Rogers had pulled it off with aplomb, as the teenaged Jackie had witnessed for herself.) Cluttered instead of classic, it pales next to the starfish, yet both are believed to have been ordered by Rogers at the same time. Both pieces now claim a seminal place in jewelry history.

For Lorian Buckley, the appeal of the starfish was more personal and primordial. "It was red and it was an animal. And starfish are such neat creatures anyhow. I was fascinated with this one made of rubies sitting in my lap." She vividly remembered playing with it before her mother wore it out the same night. Though Millicent's starfish was not as fully articulated as the other two made by Boivin, its rays had some range of movement so it would conform slightly to the contour of the wearer's body. The joints are visible from the back, and Lorian said, "The intricacy of the spiderwebbing on the back is the first thing you see when you turn it over." She saw her mother wearing it on an evening dress on several occasions but cannot remember the dress, just the starfish. As an adult, she more eloquently summarized its appeal. "The starfish is a very tactile thing and the tendrils underneath are part of it. It appealed to both senses. On one hand it looks like the sea. And looking at how it is made was also fascinating."

When her parents divorced the starfish went with her father and eventually to Jackie, his last wife. Lorian remembered seeing Jackie wearing it with a big black hat. The starfish was "big and wonderful. Not a flimsy little thing." She suspects that it was the strong impression of the starfish on her beautiful stepmother that contributed to her lack of interest in owning it later.

So when Jackie asked, "Would it crush you if I sold it?" Lorian readily deferred to her stepmother. "It was her piece, not mine, and horses are the true love in her life." She understood that the proceeds from the starfish would go toward Jackie's racehorses. Lorian also believed that she could help her to sell the jewelry. She did not want to carry it herself in a pocket up and down Fifth Avenue to jewelry dealers. "I'd be hysterical." So she went to a friend, someone whose opinion she trusted in a world that she considered to be "a slimy business." The friend mentioned Henry Baker.

Chapter Fourteen

I CAUGHT HENRY BAKER ON HIS CELL PHONE BETWEEN PALM Beach and Dallas. He proudly told me that his employer, Oscar Heyman jewelers, had been in the jewelry business for 101 years and had made the most important jewelry in America. Heyman designed diamonds for Elizabeth Taylor and his pieces figured largely in the Marjorie Merriweather estate.

Then Baker told me how he happened to get hold of Millicent Rogers's Boivin starfish. "It was a fluke." He ran through it briskly. There had been about twenty-five pieces of jewelry in the Ramos safe, he said. Some of them had belonged to Millicent. "Some were junk," he recalled, and then he had sorted out the starfish. "These pins are difficult to sell," he said. And to make matters worse in his calculation, Millicent Rogers is known "but she wasn't Liz Taylor." He said that the starfish was hard to find a buyer for in New York after he acquired it. "I dragged it all around New York," he boasted joylessly. On his first cursory rounds of touting it to jewelers, the offers were "like twenty thousand," he said. Peanuts. Chump change in the vintage jewelry business. So, he put the starfish in his pocket and took it to Europe. "Boivin and Paul Flato are common things over there, the way that Tiffany and Cartier are here," he explained.

I could tell already that Henry had a more matter-of-fact approach to jewelry than anyone I had spoken with so far. "It's a financial affair," he said flatly. I heard the dismissive shrug in his deep voice with a Texas twang. He sounded quite different from the other jewelers I had spoken to so far. It was the first time that I had heard the brooch called merely "a pin" by a jeweler. The dealers invariably called it a brooch. "Brooch," while dated, sounds somehow stately and more substantive. He led me quickly through the course that the starfish followed. "I sold it to a dealer in London who wanted the blood of Millicent Rogers as proof it was hers," he said. I assumed this was Sam Loxton, who in his own words had told me he "put it on ice for six months" while he strategized about how to best advertise and show the piece. He commissioned Claudine Seroussi to research and write about it. He took it to a jewelry show in Miami to show to Lee Siegelson. Then, as best Henry recalls, the starfish changed hands twice in the United States over the next few weeks, which suggests that it went to Stephen Russell before Lee Siegelson bought it. Lee suggested to me there had been a partnership between him and Stephen Russell. He was vague. "We've worked on a few together," Lee had said, waving his hand nonchalantly. All of these were fairly fast handoffs except for the period it was kept by Siegelson as he positioned and featured the brooch as he is apt to do when he hopes to create interest in a valuable piece.

"Everyone was laughing when Lee bought it. He paid six

fortunes for it," said Henry, who was nonetheless a bit admiring of how Lee's money enabled him to do such things. It was not urgent that he turn around and sell it immediately to recoup his purchase price. At the time we spoke, Henry did not know the piece had sold again, perhaps for those ten fortunes. And he was not inured to the piece's beauty. "The starfish looks like a starfish in its depths. I really liked them very much," he conceded, but dispassionately added, "It wasn't as finely made as you'd think. Boivin was a great Paris manufacturer, but it was a tiny shop. And after the war it got failing and sloppy. It was what it was." We did not discuss that Millicent's starfish was made before World War II. He made his point that even the great French jewelry houses were fallible and diminished with time. And as I was about to learn, they licensed "later" models of some of their best pieces to be reproduced by inferior manufacturing. *Reproductions* with pedigree.

Henry, who has worked in jewelry for forty years, came from a different point of origin than most jewelers. His background was finance. "My approach is different. For me it's only about the money. I don't want a hippo or a starfish." It was easy to like his forthright manner. He did not seem the villain that he had become in Jackie Ramos's book since she realized what her starfish was worth. And it was clear to me that he had not followed in great detail the sales history of the pieces after they left his hands. He was not romantic, and the starfish—perhaps no jewelry would— had not cast a spell over him. "Younger groups want something different. If Boivin had seven hundred pieces, I'd guess twenty percent of them are broken and gone. They get rarer and rarer every year." I could hear the *ca-ching* of the cash register in his head. The phenomenon is good for sales interest. "There is all this new wealth in the world, but the style [a brooch] is not attractive. A starfish pin without a diamond in it. No flash," he concluded. When I pressed him for his personal reaction, he deflected the question. "For me it's an investment. It's nothing I'd grab, for certain." He rattled off some trends in the jewelry business, which interested him more for their financial indicators than specific pieces did. He kept his eye on the bottom line. When we hung up I thought that he was the straightest shooter I had spoken with in the jewelry business so far.

The last thing Henry Baker told me was how quickly jewelry like the Boivin starfish could change hands once it hit the market. Typically, he explained, when he went to London he would appear with a piece of jewelry in the Burlington Arcade, where a half-dozen top jewelry stores are located. He might sell a piece in the morning and learn that by the time he awakened the following day it had changed hands more than half a dozen times again and at a substantial price jump each time. That was how fast some pieces of jewelry could move. This was news to me. I didn't know it worked that way. He told me I should go to London, where he had taken Millicent's starfish, and he rattled off the names of a handful of jewelers whom I should speak with. And then he offered me something few other jewelers had proffered. "Use my name," he said. I would.

Chapter Fifteen

NTIL I SPOKE WITH HENRY BAKER, LONDON HAD NOT figured into my notion of places where the Boivin starfish had traveled, but when he told me about setting out early in the morning with a "twenty- or forty-thousand-dollar ring" to sell, and learning the day after he'd sold it that it had exchanged hands another three times, each with a hefty price bump, my interest went way up. I was discovering that jewelry at this level is truly an international commodity, traveling casually across oceans as easily as walking down a block on Fifth Avenue. There was no reason to believe that the starfish I sought were there, but plenty of evidence that they had been seen by the jewelers who worked there. My quest was turning into a gradual accumulation of hints and reports of sightings, like the logs of birdwatchers who glimpsed a rare species flying into a thicket.

Baker also mentioned several London jewelers who had taken an interest in Boivin and the starfish in particular. Baker rattled off a number of jewelry-store names like Hancocks, and SJ Phillips, "the biggest jeweler in the world," he explained. They weren't familiar to me. London sounded like a bustling jewelry market, and when I went there I was not disappointed.

Martin Travis, a jeweler with a background in auctions, was at the top of my list. He ran Symbolic & Chase on Bond Street. Symbolic & Chase knows a good deal about Boivin. Martin told me that he had seen two ruby and amethyst Boivin starfish, but that he had never owned one. He saw his first one for sale at Christie's in Paris and then a second, which he believed was a "later" one, inflexible (which I took to mean unarticulated) in Palm Beach at the IAAF exposition in 2006, the same show I had attended years later when Lee Siegelson showed me a pair of Boivin starfish earrings and was announcing he would soon be selling Millicent Rogers's starfish brooch. That was the same year that a starfish formerly owned by Oscar de la Renta, a "later one," came up for sale at Christie's. At the time I contacted Travis, Symbolic & Chase had a diamond starfish for sale on its Web site. The diamond version lacked zing. Cupped in a yellow gold setting that held it like a slipper or cell phone cover, it no longer looked alive. I was reminded of what Lee Siegelson had told me when I had asked him if the wealthy new Asian market showed an interest in vintage jewelry. His answer was no. He explained that he couldn't sell an Asian woman a Millicent Rogers starfish. The Asian market had no cultural reference for it, the way there would be for a Chanel suit or other well-known brands. "Jewelry establishes the sense of style . . . the added sense of taste," Lee explained. Diamonds and big stones were more highly esteemed in Asia.

Henry Baker had made the rounds with the Rogers starfish, shopping it to the Burlington Arcade jewelry merchants and others before he struck gold with Sam Loxton at Lucas Rarities. London, as I was about to learn, was flush with new money, and luxury goods, jewelry among them, were selling briskly in 2014.

Vivienne Becker, the noted British jewelry historian, had spoken to me about the enduring appeal of the Boivin starfish, and she had written in one of her columns for the *Financial Times* about the emergence of a new generation of dealers who were moving antique and period jewelry, like the Boivin starfish, beyond dusty specialty shops and into a more modern arena. Her articles and comments had given me a preview of the London jewelry scene that I was about to see for myself.

Sam Loxton at Lucas Rarities personified this new generation of young jewelers. I had first met the forty-three-year-old manager of Lucas Rarities in New York City, when he was there on one of his frequent business trips. His relative youth, smooth cheeks, hip goatee, and tapered trousers spoke not only of his Englishness, but also of this emerging cohort. His specialty is Art Deco jewelry from its beginning in the 1920s to the 1970s. Lucas Rarities, nestled into an upstairs salon over Brown's restaurant in Mayfair just off Bond Street, specializes in rare period jewelry and objets d'art. His generation of London dealers has moved "upstairs," as almost all the small quality shops have. Trained as an auctioneer for Christie's, Sam now runs the London base for the Munich jewelry and gem merchant Ernst Färber. As a London jewelry insider explained to me, "Sam would not have had the money to buy the starfish, but with Dominik Biehler at Färber behind him, he could do it." What he did then boosted the value of the starfish, reflecting the trend in selling vintage jewelry today. He bought the starfish and while he strategized over the campaign he planned to mount to advertise and romanticize it, he put it "on ice." During the interim he researched the provenance of the piece, the history of the era it was created in, and self-published a handsome booklet full of glossy photos and abbreviated but well-researched text about the starfish and the splendors of other Boivin pieces. This was the dealer that Henry Baker was referring to when he mentioned someone who "wanted the blood of Millicent Rogers" as verification of the provenance of the piece. His goal was to create interest and excitement about the piece. In this starfish's case, attaching the mystique of its former owner, the glamorous Millicent Rogers, to it lent both credence and class and—the purpose of it all—added value.

In contrast to New York jewelry stores and salons, Lucas Rarities in London feels cozy. I climbed the narrow gray-carpeted stairs with a well-polished wooden banister to reach the second floor. It was both modern and homey, a bit like an art studio with its tin ceilings and beige carpeting. A pillow upholstered brightly with a Union Jack had been tossed on the couch for a splash of color.

On his own turf Sam sported jeans and seemed more harried than he had been when we met over breakfast at the Sherry-Netherland in New York several months earlier, partly, I assumed, because of the recent birth of a third child in his family and the upcoming Masterpieces London jewelry show he was preparing for in London. He was a busy guy, and he seemed a little impatient with a second round of questions about the starfish. Rather than give details about how he came by it he spoke in generalities. "It is a very expensive, very important piece," he said. He had wanted it for a show he had been mounting, Art Antiques London, three years earlier. "No one else in London had one except for me," he told me proudly. Landing a starfish in the trade was clearly an achievement to put a notch on your belt. It was also clear from my former conversation with him that he, like almost everyone who comes in true contact with the starfish, had fallen in love with it. "The scale is wonderful and the movement makes you feel like it could crawl up your arm. The workmanship is extraordinary.

It was my favorite," he said, repeating a refrain that I heard again and again both from women who wore the piece and men who for only a brief moment in time possessed it.

It was Sam, enterprising and quick on his feet, who offered Millicent's starfish to Nico Landrigan when he was visiting in New York and learned of the upcoming launch party for my biography of her at Verdura. He knew the Verdura guest and client list would expose the piece to the New York market he sought. "The piece caused a huge sensation," he claims, though that is hard to quantify. What it did do was eventually help attract one dealer who was not at the party, Lee Siegelson. Sam, like most jewelers who have handled a starfish, spoke somewhat reverently of it even after it had passed out of his hands.

Sam treaded carefully while telling his story of finding the starfish, ever protective of the client and his network of providers, but he said he first saw it when Henry Baker showed it to him. Henry offered the piece and Rogers's Boivin hippocamp brooch to Sam, presenting them for him to look at on a tabletop. Sam was bewitched with the starfish and started researching it immediately with his researcher, Claudine Seroussi, who would find her way to me some months later. "I knew it was Boivin and I knew it was rare. I had to buy it," he said with a smile. But before he committed he asked for it to be delivered to him in London where Dominik Biehler could have a look at it. The two of them decided to buy both it and the hippocamp.

As he had explained to me earlier, he kept the piece off the market to position it and build interest, bringing it out first to display at the Art Antiques London show in 2012.

While Sam and Dominik were bewitched by the starfish, its beauty and history, it was in fact the rather awkward hippocamp that was assigned a great surprise value. The little gray pearl that dangles from the bow at the bottom of the merhorse, it turned out, was extremely valuable. A half million dollars was the estimate I heard.

I stuck to the trail the starfish had followed. Although Jonathan Norton at SJ Phillips had said in his messages to me via e-mail that he didn't know anything about the Boivin starfish, I decided to pay a visit to him and his landmark store on New Bond Street. (It has since moved.) Henry Baker had been adamant that I should go there. SJ Phillips is one of the oldest family-owned antiques and jewelry dealers. He specializes in silver and estate jewelry. It had a far more venerable feeling than the Lucas Rarities aerie and was a place where you could buy a silver snuffbox or a diamond necklace. I was ushered through the long front showroom full of sparkling silver serving sets in glass cases to the back room where Jonathan sat to receive me. Impeccably dressed in a suit and tie, with shaven jowls and a florid complexion, he was the picture of British self-assuredness and jocular civility. He invited me to have a seat at his leather desk, while his brother Nicolas, taller and trimmer in a tawny summer tweed suit with his glasses dangling on a chain around his neck, looked down on us. I could see Jonathan was amused by the premise of my story. In fact, I felt that both he and Nicolas were somewhat entertained by my arrival. Jonathan declared that he had never seen a Boivin ruby and amethyst starfish and if he had, well, "I'd melt it down. It's not my kind of thing." For good measure he added that he'd never been a fan of Lalique, the French glass and jewelry designer from the same era, either. We spoke for a moment about the preference of rich Americans for diamonds today. "A bit sad, isn't it," tut-tutted Jonathan. He told me that he was well acquainted with Ward Landrigan from the time when Ward worked for Sotheby's and Jonathan had tried to teach him cricket. He raised his eyebrows with a jolly little laugh as he recalled those days. We were getting nowhere. He made it quite clear that SJ

Phillips truly had no experience with the Boivin starfish. I shouldn't have been surprised, but I was, having a bit of the girl from Indiana in me, to meet a dealer with SJ Phillips at a Christie's auction in New York eight months later who told me he had sold several Boivin starfish.

Geoffrey Munn was a name that Janet Zapata in New York had given me. She liked Munn and thought he was good at "puzzling out things" about jewelry. He worked for Wartski, the jewelers who handle the original Fabergé jewelry. Geoffrey Munn is a noted jewelry historian and gifted at articulating his views on jewelry topics with authority and simplicity. He gave me a brief summary of fine jewelry history.

In the 1900s when there was no entertainment or cinemas, he explained, there were hunts, and horseracing and the theater for fun among people with money. They dressed to the highest for dances and balls and "jewelry is the highest form of dress. It is always the essence of what else is going on. A distillation," he added. "It is a covert language full of secrets," he said. No kidding.

I walked through the Burlington Arcade, an elegant covered shopping area behind Bond Street that was created for luxury goods in the mid-nineteenth century and stretches from Piccadilly to Burlington Gardens. For fun, at every jewelry shop I stopped to ask if they had a Boivin ruby and amethyst starfish. I thought of Henry Baker coming here with a hot item to peddle in his pocket and making the rounds.

Just down the road on Piccadilly is Bentley & Skinner, another fine British jeweler with an august history. Founded in 1881 to supply jewels to the royal family, it has since been appointed as jeweler to the queen and the Prince of Wales. I am not certain what this truly means except that the crests of her majesty and the prince adorn the catalogue and publicity materials. I was met by the store's handsome and forthcoming deputy manager, Alessandro Borruso, a Sicilian. "The market is completely changed by the Internet. It is now specialty markets," he explained to me, mentioning that Bentley & Skinner's business was once based on warrants from the queen and the Prince of Wales. They also handled Lalique and Fabergé, and now, he boasted, they supplied the gems for the modern artist Damien Hirst's diamond-studded skull and a silver mirror. Just eight years ago, he told me, he was a geologist in Italy. After seeing a jewelry show he made the transition to gemology and a new career that brought him to England.

The history of Bentley & Skinner did not include Boivin, so I prepared to make my exit when Alessandro excitedly waved to his sales staff to bring the black leather box open to the diamond tiara that Lady Mary wore for her wedding in the *Downton Abbey* television series to his desk. He is rightly proud of the delicate sprays of diamonds that make it so extraordinary. Try it on, he suggested. The assistant with the white gloves who handles the piece was already coming my way. I relented. I let him snap my photo on my cell phone. It didn't make me look like Lady Mary, but it was a beautiful tiara. He pressed a small catalogue with a gold spine into my hands as I left, and I was totally amazed when I opened it back at my hotel to find that it opens not with a classic introduction about the venerable business with royal patronage but an entirely unrelated five-page story by Somerset Maugham entitled "Mr. Know-All" that tells the story of a pearl merchant who uncovers the infidelity of the wife of a fellow passenger on a transatlantic ocean liner. The jewelry business, as if I didn't already know, is *not* like other businesses.

The memory of the Rogers starfish was not completely cold among other jewelers in London. There was the hint of a trail; something unmentioned, but the cause of a little throat-clearing, had eased its way from inside Henry Baker's pocket and flitted across the desks and viewing stations of half a dozen London jewelry salons before it stopped with Sam Loxton. Stephen Burton, the principal at Hancocks, told me later when I met with him in New York that he had seen the starfish when it came through.

Martin Travis at Symbolic & Chase suggested I visit with a jeweler I had never heard of, Peter Edwards. Edwards was known for carrying Boivin pieces, and I was learning that people in the jewelry business seldom made an idle suggestion.

Visiting the Peter Edwards shop was more like paying a visit to a private home than a store. The ground-floor entrance on Conduit Street is below a discreet black-and-white sign and required ringing the doorbell. Rather than a liveried security guard waiting to let me in, Peter Edwards himself came to the door. It was covered with wrought-iron grillwork that at the hour I arrived made an interesting dappled shadow on the plush pearly gray carpet inside. Edwards looked the part of the aesthete he is, a lovely mannequin of a man, angular, smooth gray-blond hair just so, soft loafers, dark slacks, and a white silk shirt tailored and pressed to fall perfectly from the collar. Low lighting contributed to the muted mood. Small showcase boxes hung sparingly at eye level on the walls under large black-and-white glamour photos of models and famous faces wearing jewelry by the seven designers whose works were Edwards's specialty. Edwards offered me a chair across from his desk and then took his seat behind it, crossing his ankles.

He had seen a Boivin starfish, he recalled, about fifteen years ago that he thought he had heard sold for about sixty thousand British pounds. A later one sold for well over a hundred thousand in the 1990s. He thought he had seen it at the Paris Biennale.

He said that he had had a few clients come in over the years looking for a Boivin starfish, and then three years ago some women shoppers came in somewhat atwitter over one that they had seen on a woman at a luncheon in the West End. He fought for a moment to remember whose it was. "That American multibillionaire who bought a big house on Eaton Square." Then it came to him. Howard Marks. Howard Marks had entered his shop looking for a Flato piece that had articulated wings and flapped. It was his wife, Nancy, who was seen wearing the starfish out to lunch.

This was big news. Finally. The Marks starfish, because of the date, could not have been the Millicent Rogers version. This had to be one made either earlier or later.

Steeped in the history of Boivin and Belperron, Edwards reminded me, "Everybody who was anybody between 1935 and 1945 bought from Boivin." He mentioned Lady Diana Cooper and Diana Vreeland and added that the cachet of Boivin's pieces was enduring. He had sold a pair of Boivin earrings several hours before my arrival. What frustrated him, and others, is that these pieces are "certified by design, not mark." So someone could find it and copy it. Being able to recognize and differentiate the real starfish from later reproductions is what has put Françoise Cailles on center stage. Jewelers need her—somebody—to document workmanship and design that was considered by Jeanne Boivin to be all that was necessary to identify the jeweler's work. How else could they prove that the pieces of jewelry were genuine without giving prospective buyers a whole history lesson on Jeanne Boivin and the French jewelry business in the 1930s? I sympathized. Catalogue notes proudly mentioned if a piece was signed with the maker's mark or name, and in the case of the starfish included mention that Françoise Cailles had authenticated it. Like so much of the jewelry business, the logic refracted like light bouncing around in a complex cut diamond. Cold truth was hard to arrive at. What it did make clear was how Françoise Cailles had achieved eminence in her role as the sole authenticator of Boivin. Jewelers needed her because without her authentication, there was always a question. I began to think that there was room for a small degree of uncertainty even with her authentication, but she was what we had. She admitted that there were very few stock books. "Most of Boivin's jewels were commissioned pieces, to be delivered unsigned as soon as they were completed," Cailles explained.

Edwards made a gentle swerve in our conversation. The upcoming Masterpiece London show was evidently on his mind. Like many jewelers I encountered, he spoke admiringly and enviously of Lee Siegelson. "Lee buys it for one hundred or two hundred and sells it for a million," he said hyperbolically, giving me a tight smile. He understood that was roughly what he had done with the Rogers starfish.

I finally had the opportunity in London to meet Claudine Seroussi, the most knowledgeable researcher for Sam Loxton who had contacted me about Millicent's starfish when Sam was mounting his campaign with a well-researched booklet on Boivin that included the starfish. Claudine had been a bright light among the people I had encountered in the jewelry world, a personality on e-mail willing to make suggestions and direct my inquiries. Her knowledge of jewelry history was nearly encyclopedic and by the time we met in London she was studying for her degree in gemology. I was anxious to meet her. We had spoken once before on Skype and to my chagrin our whole interview had been on camera. Sitting at home in New Mexico, juggling a nine-hour time difference between us, I was wearing pajamas. Even on a Skype camera I could see the thumb-sized emerald ring she wore.

Claudine, like all jewelers, was cautious. But very helpful. She spoke of the genesis of naturalism in jewelry design as it affected Jean Schlumberger of Tiffany & Co., and Boivin. And she explained to me that a piece of jewelry could not get an assay mark in France without being made in a workshop of French jewelers.

The mark was a very controlling sort of documentation, even though after a piece was purchased the owner might go to some lengths to have it removed to avoid taxes. She knew where the human element intersected the business.

Claudine's expert eye had also found a small clue that might explain the elusiveness of the third starfish's trail. It was in a book about exhibition jewels published for the Victoria and Albert Museum by its curator Graham Hughes in 1962. An image of a Boivin starfish and a famous Boivin chameleon are photographed side by side. On the line with the letter *o* to indicate the owner's name is the name Boivin, suggesting that in 1968, when the final edition of the book was published, one ruby and amethyst starfish was—news again—*still owned by Boivin!* This third early starfish was becoming a tantalizing mystery, making an appearance and then disappearing. It was not Millicent Rogers's. No one, in my inquiries, so far, had claimed any knowledge of it. But it was out there. Where was it now?

In my rounds I had become inured to the chorus of praises that dealers sang to the starfish, but the London jewelers reminded me of their significance. Everyone knew of these famous pieces. Most had seen them whether they had owned them or not. Sam Loxton had studiously explained their historical importance. "They heralded the advent of the three-dimensional yellow-gold jewelry of baroque proportions that became fashionable during the 1940s and 1950s." But no one would attribute a starfish's attraction solely to good looks. There was a mystique.

Beauty, breeding, craftsmanship, value, and a string of celebrated owners contributed to it equally. I got it. I understood the appeal and aggregate value of the Boivin starfish. What I needed to find out now was where they had traveled on their peregrinations from Paris, on whose shoulders and in whose luggage and pockets. I felt as if I had so far been following a trail of crumbs, checking in on Henry Baker's clients who had seen the starfish, leading me onward. They led to the places where Millicent Rogers's starfish had touched bottom, if only briefly, but it was the hint of two new leads that cheered me. I needed to find Howard and Nancy Marks. I wondered if their starfish might be the one that Claudette Colbert had owned. Equally intriguing was the suggestion that Boivin had held on to a starfish at least until 1968.

Chapter Sixteen

AND SO, ON TO PARIS WITH SOME APPREHENSION. I had known from the beginning that my pursuit of starfish would take me there. In addition to all the other good reasons to go, it's where Françoise Cailles, the woman who is thought to know the most about Boivin, lives and works. She is the undisputed authenticator of all Boivin jewelry pieces that come up for sale at auction and in jewelry houses, and she has written the only book, *René Boivin: Jeweller* (Quartet, 1994), about the history of the salon. Part of it is a catalogue of Boivin jewelry. The English edition sells for close to $5,000 from Amazon. Fortunately, Colleen Caslin, the chief financial officer at Verdura, loaned me her copy. I turned its pages carefully, protected its thick spine, and kept it close at hand on my desk.

Françoise Cailles had the reputation of being nearly impossible to make a date with and unresponsive to queries, a distinction that she lived up to when I contacted her. I wrote to her in French and English, by e-mail and post, at addresses provided by jewelry dealers in New York. Though I had been told that she spoke good English, I hired a Frenchwoman to translate my letter of introduction to her. In it I explained about the book I was writing and that I would come to France to meet with her at her convenience. She did not reply. It did not help that everyone who knew her said I should not take her silence personally, that this was how she operated. First I fretted, and then as months wore on I despaired. Her input was essential. I needed to speak with experts about Boivin and the French jewelry business in Paris and in London. Her failure to respond loomed large and dampened my confidence. It became an outsized anxiety. I telephoned Cailles's home and left a message in my poor French with a woman, a housekeeper I imagined, who answered. Then I bought a plane ticket and consulted with an American friend who spoke perfect French. He agreed to telephone Madame Cailles on my behalf. He telephoned me back within the same hour. She was charming, quite lovely, over the phone, he bubbled. She told him that of course, she was meeting with me. *Mais oui.* Had I not gotten her e-mail about having lunch? I had not. When I e-mailed her later the same day she replied with a time and place for our appointment. I was too relieved to wonder what had happened to that e-mail.

I arrived in Paris happy to be getting close, at last, to the early story of the starfish and to the people who could tell me more about Boivin. I also felt some trepidation about conversing in my unsatisfactory French. Sure, I could speak with the hotel concierge and tell a taxi driver where I wanted to go, but the gentle nuance that makes a story come to life or the quick follow-up question that probes memory were out of my reach in the French language. These limitations were on my mind during the cab ride to the home and studio of the Baroness Marie-Caroline de Brosses in Porte de Saint-Cloud, just outside the Paris city limits. I had stumbled upon the existence of Baroness de Brosses in conversation with a jewelry researcher early in my quest. The baroness was reputed to have an encyclopedic memory of many Boivin designs and the distinction of being the last designer in Paris who had worked with the Boivin team before the salon shuttered its doors after being sold to the venerable British jewelry firm Asprey in 1991. For whatever reason, she is hardly mentioned in Françoise Cailles's book on Boivin. I was delighted when she responded to my letter to her and agreed to speak with me. There were few people left to talk to about the Boivin story.

I took a deep breath standing outside the painted blue door to her apartment at the back of a courtyard before ringing the bell. Wearing tight blue flowered jeans and heels, she opened the door. *"Bonjour,"* she said with the customary hi-lo chime the French give to it and then "you are here" in English that assured me we would be able to converse in English. I breathed a sigh of relief. Her small but nicely appointed living room was decorated with white ceramic elephant lamps under pink shades and upholstered blue velvet furniture. She ushered me to a seat on the blue couches with tassled fringe skirts. A Boivin silver and gold diamond cat pendant the size of a silver dollar hung on her chest. She later told me she was wearing it on my behalf. After a polite pause for pleasantries, Perrier and strawberries, de Brosses told me the story of going to work for Boivin in 1970. I felt her decompress as she talked about being a young designer in her twenties. Perhaps the reason she is largely missing from accounts of the House of Boivin is explained in part because she missed the company's heyday, yet she clearly enjoys telling the story of going to the salon on the Avenue de l'Opéra for the first time. In her account it was a dusty place with shutters, past its prime. The comedy in the scene she created made her laugh. She loved the manager, "the wonderful Monsieur

Girard, very old," who cranked open the shutters, making dust motes in the air visible in the dim light. She recalled the old woman called the "angel" in jewelry shop parlance who sat at the front door and did the accounts. The angel was also the secretary, and strung pearls from her high stool perch, once a regular fixture in Parisian jewelry houses. "So cute, old ladies with curly white hair and hunched over their work," de Brosses remembered. The Boivin daughters, *"filles"* as they were called, though they were mature women by then, came every day to the salon for tea.

And then her story took a little curve and she picked her words carefully. She was delighted, she explained, to be offered the job designing for Boivin and she was charmed by Monsieur Girard, "but I still had Juliette." She sighed. "Of course, she was threatened by me." It was apparent to de Brosses that the aging Moutard resented her presence, and though they worked together on three or four different designs to show to a client, "when they were presented, Juliette wouldn't credit me." She resented that the older woman did not teach her more. She can see her still, wearing "a smock like a chem lab coat." There was no love lost between them. During the eight months they worked side by side at Boivin, de Brosses, who was transitioning from a study of architecture, began to draw what she liked. Her work, she said, was considered to be new, on the cusp of change. After a rough first year, her tenure at Boivin stretched to twenty years.

The days of Moutard's brilliant successes with the starfish and other maritime motifs were over, but as a student of the salon's past and her design predecessors, de Brosses arrived at some conclusions about the two women's work. "Suzanne Belperron had muscle. She may well have had the starfish idea first. Juliette was soft. She came from working on small clocks, that was her world." But whatever ingredients were part of the alchemy for jewelry design greatness, de Brosses is the only one who can recount the creative atmosphere at Boivin. "They were very eccentric!" she says, speaking of all the women, including Madame Boivin and her daughter Germaine, who "collected bones in the forest and shells and glued them together." In her recollection, the salon and workplace were a sort of magic shop, or an enchanted forest of women making jewelry. They pushed the edges of naturalistic whimsy. Their license to tinker, to muse and create, would change in the 1980s when work began to be priced by the hour. In her estimation a starfish would have required eighty hours of work, design through fabrication. "Like the advent of brands, this was a big change," she explained.

There were little things that distinguished the rarefied life at the house. "Lapidary in the old days was done by color or provenance." Rubies from Burma, though a lovely hue of red, were of poor quality. "But we cared more about color." It was how a piece looked from an artistic standpoint that counted at Boivin. Monsieur Girard had a thumb-sized emerald that seemed to have herbs visible in its gem formation. The imperfection would have disqualified it for setting in the estimation of some more conservative jewelers. "We didn't care," de Brosses told me, exhibiting the swashbuckling confidence of designers who ranked style above sheer quality. What struck me was how this small jewelry house became eminent for quality and design, getting it right enough times to hold a place in both worlds without sacrificing one at the expense of the other.

There was also the plain old fun and risqué gossip of a French jewelry salon. When I asked her to tell me about the mood and atmosphere of the Boivin salon that she had experienced, she told me a story that captured a different era in French history. A client who worked for a big bank in Paris came to the salon to see the manager, Monsieur Girard. The man was impeccably groomed in a suit and neat tie, the uniform of a rich French banker. He shopped with swagger and bought a necklace of rubies and diamonds that he asked to have wrapped as a gift. To the surprise of the Boivin staff he returned to the salon after lunch a total mess. His fly was unzipped, his tie was akimbo, de Brosses remembers. The client told Monsieur Girard, "She did not want it." Yet by the looks of him, it had not dulled her ardor. De Brosses started laughing before she got the last few words out of her mouth and we giggled over such ludicrousness together. Those were apparently the days of French high-flying and there were many such occurrences at Boivin. She took me back to the Belperron days at Boivin in the early thirties and told that story of the legendary designer showing stones to her clients in a long upturned fingernail. I was uncertain whether this was merely eccentric or creepy.

De Brosses knew a little about the progression of design that led to the starfish. It was her understanding that Suzanne Belperron made some designs that included starfish and that during this period Madame Boivin asked for shell designs from her. After Belperron left it was Juliette who continued and excelled with the maritime motif, especially the Boivin starfish. De Brosses had always had the impression that five were made in the thirties and forties, perhaps not all of them ruby and amethyst.

De Brosses provided some insight into the source of Cailles's expertise on the House of Boivin. Cailles's husband, Michel Perinet, was a brilliant antiques merchant with a renowned eye for almost anything of age. De Brosses recalled that he bought a painting in a Boivin sale that sold for ten times his purchase price five years later. Lee Siegelson had mentioned to me that he had first seen a starfish in 1992, I thought at Perinet. Perinet and his wife Françoise's history and expertise with Boivin are intertwined with the Boivin starfish's story.

De Brosses was absolute about the difference between Belperron and Boivin starfish. She found them easy to differentiate. I had not seen a Belperron starfish, except in drawings. With her expert eye, she could tell that Belperron's stones were set in a more modern fashion, and her starfish designs, older than Juliette

Moutard's, "had little points and smaller flips at the end." In the drawings I have seen they are more uniform and geometric, whereas Moutard's seem like live creatures.

De Brosses was still actively designing jewelry. During my visit to her an assistant and student arrived to head upstairs to her workshop. I was relieved to have started my reporting in Paris with her. She buoyed my confidence. The next day was my lunch date with Cailles.

I had heard from everyone in the jewelry business whom I asked about the Boivin starfish that I must meet with Cailles and that she was most likely to have the answers I was looking for, but I was also told that some of her assertions and authentications were open to challenge. Sam Loxton at Lucas Rarities had told me that Cailles had "volumes and volumes of daybooks and ledgers. They were bought from Asprey." Asprey was the last owner of Boivin before it closed its doors. It seemed to be the classic story of a large conglomerate wanting the brand Boivin and the status the name conferred, but once it owned it, the parent company could not maintain the quality or accept the profit margins of a small operation.

It is undisputed that the archives—and the rights to replicate jewelry from them—are owned by Nathalie Hocq, but Cailles seems to have sufficient access to or perhaps copies that enable her to fulfill her duties of authentication. She steadfastly refuses to show what she has, or as she explains most things, they are a *secret*.

To put it a bit inelegantly, Françoise Cailles is the troll at the bridge of the market in Boivin jewelry. Only she can authenticate pieces created by Boivin, and her certification is needed for a sale. This service is offered for a fee. The library Loxton referred to is evidently the one that is used to authenticate the pieces Cailles is called upon to vouch for, but she does not show it to others. This lack of visible documentation and drawings frustrates dealers who have pieces for sale and have one owner or one source to prove their provenance. Some of her decisions, I am told, have been shown to be incorrect or reversed later, especially when they have been made based on photographs instead of seeing a piece. Of the hundreds of pieces of Boivin jewelry she has ruled on, it seems forgivable to have made a few mistakes, but the lack of public documentation or alternate evidence of authentication beyond her nod aggravates jewelers. And there is an additional complication: while there are whispers of a few errors, no one wants to be on record pointing them out publicly, because to challenge Cailles's supremacy as an authenticator could bring down the hierarchy on which past sales and current prices were valued. In the world of fine jewelry all pretenses and postures are preserved, even if proved incorrect, when it's a matter of money. And it always is.

Adding to the difficulty of knowing about the history and origins of French jewelry is the habit that fine pieces have of disappearing for long periods of time, either because they reside innocently in the collection of a long-forgotten owner, or because they are acquired and kept in deep secrecy. Millicent Rogers's starfish stayed in her family for seventy-five years. The "third" Boivin starfish seems to have been held in the dark by its creators and owners for decades. Sometimes jewelry as fine as Boivin's pieces was kept within a family for several generations. When I spoke with French jewelers and owners, they would have liked for me to accept that this was the fate of all fine jewelry in France. The instinct to avoid having one's wealth known publicly and to evade estate and inheritance taxes makes the French go to great lengths to keep their jewelry secret. "You don't want to ever talk to a French woman about her jewelry," an American dealer of vintage French pieces warned me, when I shared my intentions with her.

This tendency, compulsion really, was explained to me by Jean

Pierre Brun, the man whose family for years had a leading jewelry workshop in Paris that produced roughly a quarter of Boivin's designs. He is connected with Profillet, the name of the workshop that made the original starfish. Brun is of an age and type of Parisian man who still kisses a lady's hand when they meet and sounds like Maurice Chevalier when he talks. He is full of lore about the old days in French jewelry making. He explained to me that I must take into account the true nature of French people for my story. "They are different," he said of the French owners of jewelry like the starfish. "They don't show off. If you have a nice big car here, you hide it." Such instinct was perhaps more practical than cultural since the French "wealth tax" that assesses French citizens' wealth annually and taxes them accordingly is a mighty incentive for secrecy.

Brun and I were talking in the lobby of my hotel on Rue Madame in Paris, coincidentally the same street where he has lived his entire life. I was reminded that jewelry artisans occupied a social position well above tradesmen in twentieth-century France. Their status was more like that of fashion designers in the United States today. Brun told me that he spoke almost every day to Nathalie Hocq Choay, the woman who now owns the Boivin brand. She bought it when Asprey, then owned by the billionaire playboy Prince Jefri Bolkiah, brother of the Sultan of Brunei, sold it in something of a fire sale, to cover his debts, making her the owner of the archives and adding the remaining inventory to her jewelry store Poiray on the Rue de la Paix in Paris, according to Brun. Poiray was dedicated to making fine jewelry for a younger clientele at a lower price point than the old flagship brands, something Hocq had championed at Cartier. She was of keen interest to me because owning the brand meant she had whatever archives remained from Boivin. These would include sales records and design orders. I had written and phoned her, but without results. Brun promised to ask her to speak with me. He had first

been suggested to me by Ralph Esmerian, the previous owner of
Fred Leighton jewelry in New York, who was then serving a prison
term for fraud. He kept in touch with Ralph.

Who else would he suggest I speak to? I asked. I ended every
interview by asking that. "Have you talked to Murray?" he asked.
Ah yes, Murray Mondschein again.

I met Françoise Cailles for our appointed lunch date at the
restaurant of her choosing, Ladurée, on the Left Bank. "Very
French," she had described it in her e-mail of confirmation to me.
I wondered if she knew it had sprouted a chain of popular *macaron*
stores in New York City. One of three Ladurée restaurants in Paris,
the tearoom on Rue Bonaparte is a bustling full-scale restaurant,
not just the patisserie it is known for in the United States. The
muraled walls, full of monkeys and palm trees, circle the downstairs dining room, but the maître d' led me upstairs to a quieter,
buffeted room. The woman who rose to meet me in trousers and
a copper-colored blazer did not look like the dragon lady I had
begun to imagine. Her chestnut hair was stylishly coiffed and she
looked younger than an online photo I had seen of her with a group
of French jewelry advisers. She wore minimal jewelry, small gold
earrings and a chain. I took my seat on a deep blue velvet ban-
quette with a tasseled hem. Curtains pulled aside with a matching
swag framed windows that looked onto the street below. Yes, very
French, I thought, more like American fantasies of restaurants for
assignations. The clatter of glassware and silver below was at a dis-
tance and I was grateful that the room where we sat was reason-
ably quiet.

Cailles nearly whispered when she talked of the history of
Boivin. I was straining to make out her mix of English and French,
but I recorded our conversation. Everything she said was cryptic.
Ah, when I asked about the sales ledgers for Boivin, "The record
is not complete," she said. I had already heard that she never

produces anything to peruse for anyone who is researching Boivin pieces. Everything depends on her memory, unseen notes, and her assertion.

As for learning the names of the owners of the starfish, at least the third one whose original buyer was unknown to me, she explained, "You can only be told the name of the person in France when it was published." I take this to mean that after someone else has published it first, or perhaps when the owner dies. "Boivin and its society were private," she said flatly, and as our lunch was served she continued with something of a lecture on the culture of this privacy. "*Bijoux* are always something very personal, very expensive. It is high society," she said, believing that she had made her point. I wondered, watching her carefully, if she really thought that I had come five thousand miles to hear this.

When I inquired if she had known someone who had a starfish whom I could speak to, her expression was of controlled horror. Her eyes darted at our fellow diners. It was as if I had asked something extremely personal and unsavory, coarse even. This whole business of asking direct questions, I could see, was not getting me very far. I watched her absorb and reckon with the idea of a book such as this about jewelry and people. It was a foreign concept to her. "This could never happen in France," she told me, unblinking, as though that was enough said. I tried another tack and asked if it is less sensitive to speak of the prices or the pieces of jewelry instead of owners. Weren't ledgers kept? *Oui.* "Ah yes, they were," she said, "but of course, they were in code." *Code?* Just about everything I had found out so far had begun to feel like code to me.

Cailles claimed she didn't know the price that Boivin's pieces sold for because the record books were coded and she doesn't know the code. This is hard for me to grasp or to accept, but our conversation moved on. She continued her whispered incantations on the meaning of jewelry in France. *Jewels are the pride of the family . . . They stay in the family until death.*

Cailles continued to talk generalities. She invited me to come to Paris again for longer. She was amazed that I declined the glass of champagne that the waiter offered, yet she did the same. When I said no to dessert she insisted I have a *macaron*. I began to feel that I was being treated like an ingénue tourist, someone that would be swayed from her mission by a little bubbly and a French pastry, just happy to be there. I asked whom she would advise me to talk with in New York about the starfish. She knew that I had already seen Ward Landrigan at Verdura and Lee Siegelson since they had referred me to her. "Murray Mondschein, I think, knows about them," she said. Always Murray.

She went on to say that during my next visit I must come to her house, a *hôtel particulier* or mansion, that I had already heard much about. Perinet, her husband, had been one of the leading antique furniture and jewelry dealers in Paris, and their home, dark and richly furnished, had made an impression on anyone who had seen it. I had also been told that it was Perinet who suggested to his wife to write the book about Boivin when he learned that the last owner of Boivin, Jacques Bernard, who presided over it after he sold to Asprey, wanted a book written. Thus she had become the expert on Boivin. I began to think grudgingly that this encounter would be the first of several, just the icebreaker to introduce us. She asked if I would agree to practice English with her on my next, longer trip. This sounded good and felt unlikely. She had not been especially forthcoming, and I could see that the whole concept of a book about the owners and movement of jewelry through people's lives was an alien notion to her. She had already told me that she could not imagine it. "Never in France," she said adamantly, bringing a forkful of salad to her mouth. We parted on the street outside the restaurant, her arms filled with books like a schoolgirl. She was going to Tajan, one of the best French auction houses, where she works in the vintage jewelry department. It had been a lovely lunch, on the level of lunches. But I had hoped she would help me enter the world where the mysteries of the starfish are kept. On that level, the score was clearly Françoise 1, Cherie 0. The charming troll was victorious, the bridge still uncrossed.

Chapter Seventeen

AFTER LUNCH WITH CAILLES, I TOO TRAVELED OVER to the Right Bank, to the Musée des Arts Décoratifs to meet Evelyne Possémé, the chief curator and head of the Art Deco and jewelry department. I had been told that she is one of the world's leading experts in twentieth-century jewelry, and I was anxious to speak with an academic after reaching the limits of information to be garnered in the world of New York jewelry dealers. I had also heard that she can be gruff and does not tolerate fools, so I was a bit anxious. Even Cailles, when I took leave and told her where I was heading, echoed this sentiment. "She can be difficult," she said, smiling and striding away.

There was work going on in the museum when I arrived and I was guided up narrow spiral stairs that were veiled to protect the floor and pieces below from construction dust and debris. The museum space felt otherworldly, shrouded in misty hues and filtered light. Possémé, to my surprise, seemed more Germanic than French with her short-cut hair and clipped English. Her earnest and direct approach was comforting after Cailles's gentle dodges and hedges. Possémé furrowed her brow at my questions and reached for volumes from the library of books and texts that were scattered on the tables and shelves in an upstairs office that felt like a garret, with windows that opened more to the sky than onto the beautiful grounds of the Tuileries that I knew lay below. She told me that she first saw a starfish in 1995, at a Schlumberger fashion and jewelry event. We talked a bit about the attraction of fish, dolphins, and maritime life for Renaissance painters and for jewelers in the period of Boivin.

She then went on to explain the jewelers' marks that identified the workshops where the pieces of jewelry had actually been made. Like so many other practices I was encountering, I found that deception, often intended, was built into the identifying elements of jewelry design. The workshops that actually fabricated the pieces of jewelry from the designs that came to them from designers in jewelry houses like Boivin each had marks that would identify which shop had done the work. Much like a coat of arms, a symbol usually identified the designer and the workshop. Boivin's symbol was a snake, but Possémé told me that she had never seen it on a piece of jewelry. We both knew the story that Jeanne Boivin, like Suzanne Belperron, did not like signing or marking pieces from Boivin because she wanted their design alone to be enough to identify them. Yet workshops still lay claim with their *poinçons*, hallmarks, stamped to their work. A fine piece of jewelry could have several such brands on it, both the fabricator's stamp or signature and the designer's, always almost microscopically small. Charles Profillet made and signed Boivin's early starfish. Deception would come into the picture when pieces that lacked a mark were sent to France to be given ones that would boost their value in the United States. Alternately, buyers in France who wanted to avoid paying taxes on the pieces had the maker's marks removed, adding to the confusion. I had heard several times about how these practices made it difficult to identify original pieces from later copies by their marks alone. And I had also been told by a New York jeweler that she had once traveled to Paris to get a mark put onto a piece that lacked one. In her case, she swore, she was getting the stamp to prove the origin of a Boivin piece (you, gentle reader, and I know now that Boivin didn't use its mark, but not everyone understands that), but her story illustrated how simple it could be to acquire a mark on a reproduction. Like so many practices in the jewelry world, a convention that was meant to be helpful in learning the provenance and identification of a piece had been tampered with and was confusing

I wanted to know about the codes in sales books and ledgers that Madame Cailles had mentioned to me over lunch. The subject hit a nerve with Possémé and she seemed as interested in it as I was. She explained that most jewelers would not write the true name of a client in their books or the price of an item for sale. They created a code of nine characters that only a few principals in their own business knew. The example she used to explain this to me was of jewelers from the town of Ratisbone, Germany. She wrote the name on a yellow Post-it note for me and beneath the letters put the numbers 1 to 9. Using letters for numbers—*r* for 1, *a* for 2, *t* for 3, and so on—the jewelry house could record prices with letters and names by using numbers that were unintelligible to anyone except themselves. If a disgruntled employee left, somewhat as Suzanne Belperron had defected from Boivin to start her own business, the client lists and sales histories remained secret with the original holder. Both buyers and sellers could evade taxes, sales and perhaps inheritance, without records. "They didn't want anybody to know the price or that it changed for different clients,"

Possémé explained. This was all further evidence of how deeply ingrained secrecy is in the jewelry trade. I was beginning to understand how this culture of secrecy still coursed through the veins of the modern-day jewelry business, from Paris to, gosh, maybe even—Indiana? I hadn't tried to buy a vintage diamond ring there lately.

With details of a brooch made by another workshop that measured 6.2 by 1.45 centimeters, Possémé estimated the markup for a piece like the Boivin starfish. She guessed that the starfish sold for twice what it had cost to make.

The French, and perhaps jewelers worldwide, played endless games to obfuscate any details about their wares and markets. The French government has tried to regulate some aspects of the jewelry trade. For instance, when a design is "retired," the drawing of it is stamped (like a notary seal) with a registered number. I had seen such a stamp online on the page of a design of a Boivin starfish when the Parisian jewelry house of Pierre Bergé stopped recreating Boivin's starfish in 2011. It was the strongest evidence so far of some attempt to regulate and control a business in which it is easy to pirate creative property. And it was a record that something had occurred even when the people involved denied it. I had contacted the Pierre Bergé auction house after I was told that Mr. Bergé and Nathalie Hocq Choay in Switzerland, who now owns the Boivin archives, had made a few new starfish during the past decade. I received word from the PB's representative that Pierre Bergé knew nothing about the Boivin starfish even though she allowed that "Boivin jewels have been sold through his auction house." But the stamp on the page of the design, a retiring of the license to produce it, clearly suggested otherwise. *C'est la vie.*

The corporate offices of Van Cleef & Arpels are in the Bourse in Paris, where it is an adventure finding and then gaining entry to buildings. No outer sign advertises the businesses within. The sleek, modern, low-key reception lobby, and turnstiles through the next doorway, come as a surprise. It is like stepping into another, more modern movie. Nicholas Luchsinger, international retail director and "heritage collection" specialist for Van Cleef & Arpels, met me with a ready smile. A bounce in his quick stride and a few unruly strands that stuck out from his otherwise smooth dark hair like a cowlick lent him a boyish open charm as he settled at his desk in a clean, minimally furnished white office. After the dark entry hall on the ground floor and a haze on the Paris streets that morning, the Van Cleef offices felt like a cloud of suffused light.

Luchsinger had worked with Van Cleef for nine years and was prepared to give me an overview of the jewelry-collecting habits in France. He explained that high inheritance taxes force many families to hold on to their jewelry and add to the importance of secret-keeping. He thought he remembered seeing a Boivin starfish roughly ten years before. He mentioned that estate jewelry and jewelry auctions were a relatively new phenomenon in the world of fine jewelry, and he attributed the fashionability of estate jewelry in the 1980s to the New York jewelry store Fred Leighton. There it was again, the mention of Murray Mondschein, aka Fred Leighton. I had heard from several jewelers in New York and Paris about the role of Fred Leighton in the evolution of the jewelry business and the fame of the Boivin starfish in particular. Nicholas Luchsinger, who knows his history, thought it likely the Boivin starfish had been made sequentially, with the first one to show to prospective customers. That's probably the one Claudette Colbert bought. And the second was created to replace it. Maybe that's the one Boivin held on to until 1968. The others, including Rogers's version, were likely to have been special orders. That was his opinion.

Luchsinger went on about the enduring appeal of certain old

pieces from the thirties and forties, including the Boivin starfish and Van Cleef's ballerinas, brooches fashioned like delicate little dolls in classic ballet poses with rose-cut diamond faces and stones reputedly salvaged from Spanish crown jewels that were auctioned off in Mexico. Those little diamond dancers did not appeal to me, but I had to admit that everything about jewelry was typically made more interesting by the story that went along with it.

I was hoping that Luchsinger could help me with another piece in the riddle of the starfish. Lee Siegelson had told me a beguiling story about encountering the Millicent Rogers starfish after he had sold it. He said he did not know who the final owner was. Like most jewelers I had spoken to, he winced a little when talking about the piece moving on and out of his possession, even when the sale had been profitable for him. The Rogers starfish sold for somewhere between $800,000 and $1 million, I knew. I asked Lee if he had ever seen it again and he told me about going to Paris some months later for the Van Cleef exhibition. He said that during the champagne reception he caught a glimpse of the starfish on a woman's lapel across the room. I asked him a dozen questions about who the woman was, what she was wearing, was she blond or brunette, young or old, and so on. He seemed quite honestly not to know the answers. He thought the suit it was pinned to was black. All he remembered, like a former suitor catching a glimpse of an old love, was the starfish. "It was wonderful to see it again," he said sincerely. Then the crowd shifted and closed behind the woman who wore it, and she and her starfish vanished from sight.

I told Luchsinger this story in hopes that he would recall a Van Cleef client who might own the starfish. With his elbows on his desk he seemed to ponder. We looked through the pages of some of the Van Cleef catalogues on his conference table and then it came to him. He thought he knew who had bought the Rogers starfish. Of course, I had to understand, he said, that he couldn't tell me without her permission. I asked if she was an American. Yes, he said. In New York? Yes. Then I watched him tighten. That was all he could tell me. When I pressed, he agreed to ask if she would be willing to speak with me. Just the prospect of locating the owner of the Rogers starfish elated me.

Besides Jean Pierre Brun, there was another man in Paris, Olivier Baroin, who I hoped could shed light on the provenance of the starfish design, and the fuzzy area of influence and credit for it shared between Suzanne Belperron and Juliette Moutard. Olivier Baroin had told me that he didn't know enough about Boivin to be of interest to me when I contacted him before my trip to Paris, but he agreed to meet with me when I insisted. He was then the owner of a somewhat disputed archive of Belperron, a story I had heard rumblings about in New York, and I didn't want to get involved in it.

He met me at the Saut du Loup outdoor café nestled behind the Musée des Arts Décoratifs. "Loup," I knew, is French for wolf, which made me again recall Susan Abeles's caution that jewelers are wolves. Olivier was almost an hour late, which, instead of frustrating me as it usually would, gave me the chance to catch my breath and recover from the fatigue of straddling two languages. A handsome forty-five-year-old, he arrived in purple jeans and a white shirt wearing a cabochon ruby ring with a stone the size of a dime. He plopped two cell phones and a computer on the table between us. When I commented on his ring he explained that it was Indian, of uncertain value, and that he wore it for no better reason than that he liked it. He insisted that I try it on. I had learned by then to acquiesce. I wore it like a talisman for the rest of our interview. It was a smashing ring.

I was not surprised to learn that he had seen Madame Cailles that afternoon, following our interview. New York, London, Paris—the jewelry world is small in these cities. Everyone knows everyone, it seems. I could not resist asking him if Cailles mentioned our lunch. "Ah yes," he said, and with a grin added, "She found you very American. You ask a lot of questions," he said. I tried to share a little laugh with him. "What am I supposed to do? I came here to ask questions," I explained. He did a quick little humorous spoof of what might be acceptable. "Would you mind if perhaps I might ask you about something . . ." We shared a sigh of camaraderie and moved on.

Olivier had distinguished himself by putting all of the Belperron archives that he has onto his computer. He professed that he believed in transparency, though he explained that it is not the French or jewelry world's way. He knew the young assistant who had worked for Belperron to help her burn seventy percent of her drawings and files in the fireplace of her Paris apartment before her death. Belperron was determined not to reveal her clients, and like Boivin, she was convinced her designs were adequate to identify her work, so she didn't sign her pieces.

Baroin, who began working in jewelry workshops at the age of fourteen, is another example of someone totally enamored with jewelry and his work in the business. "I love it. It is always fascinating," he said, scrolling through his files to try to find a record of a Millicent Rogers sale, another of Daisy Fellowes. "The secrecy business," he scoffed. "Françoise would never show you anything. I try to be transparent." He wanted to set himself apart. The problem was that his expertise is Belperron. He told me he loved all designs by Belperron and that he suspected that Belperron originated the starfish motif for Jeanne Boivin, but he did not claim that the one I was following, the particular Boivin starfish, was not Juliette Moutard's. Whoever began toying with the starfish motif, this Boivin starfish seemed unquestionably to have been Moutard's. That was a relief. Baroin was also more forthcoming when talking about cost and value. Based on other pieces that sold in his archive records, he estimated that the starfish cost about

70,000 French francs, 48,000 for the stones and 15,000 for the workshop and labor cost. It is likely they sold for between FF 70,000 and FF 100,000 at the time. In "old" francs. In the 1930s the French franc was at its lowest against the dollar, one franc fluctuating in value between five and ten cents. If Olivier's estimate was correct, the starfish sold for $3,500 to $5,000, the equivalent of $60,000 to $86,000 today. He knew that Millicent Rogers paid FF 67,290 for a pansy flower brooch from Belperron, and he also knew from the record books that she was regarded as a difficult client. "Not everyone behaved like that," wanting to return things later for designs more current, and so on. I was not surprised. That was Millicent. There was not much more he could tell me about the starfish.

I walked back to my hotel across the Tuileries on a June evening that seemed to last forever; the sun stayed high so long. I was exhausted after a long day but I wanted a moment to revel in the feeling of a Parisian evening and to imagine what it must have been like for the stylish women who came to adorn themselves with what they considered the most stylish and luxurious jewelry in the world. Their era was over, but it was still possible to conjure up a whiff of that spell. Paris was and is such a place. It still does that.

Nicholas Luchsinger had put me in touch with François Curiel, the man who heads Christie's international jewelry business, and who he felt certain had overseen auctions of Boivin starfish. I had heard of Curiel, who is known for his good looks, dash, and charm to spare, as well as his willingness to go to great lengths for access to private collections for sale. "Waltzing with dowagers" was the phrase one jeweler jokingly used. It was a euphemism. Curiel is a legendary name in the business, credited mainly with overhauling the auction business from a forum that catered mostly to the trade to a public exchange.

Curiel's account of the business made it easier to understand how rare pieces like the Boivin starfish move in and out of international auctions in New York, Paris, and Geneva, the three most important auction hubs. The auctions become anonymous revolving doors for sellers and shoppers. Curiel also provided me with the listings for four Boivin starfish that Christie's sold between 1996 and 2010. He could not remember, or wouldn't reveal, anything more about them. With the thousands of jewels that had passed through Christie's under his watch, it was hard to imagine that he had any personal recollection of the sale of the brooches even though they invariably made an impression on whoever saw them. I had come to accept that there were four, and maybe even five, original Boivin ruby and amethyst starfish brooches moving through the universe.

As I packed to leave Paris I realized that while the cast of colorful *Parisiens* had been informative and entertaining, I was leaving with only one new trail to follow. I was hopeful that the Van Cleef client who was the new owner of Millicent Rogers's starfish would agree to speak with me. Clues about the whereabouts of the starfish were discouragingly hard to come by. It was something.

Chapter Eighteen

N PARIS I HAD GOTTEN A BETTER UNDERSTANDING OF THE starfish's creators and their European dealers, but I hadn't helped myself much further down the trails the brooches had taken. Back in the States, though, it seemed my luck was changing. After a year of asking questions and starting to find my way around jewelers in New York, I realized that the names of a few private collectors came up repeatedly in conversation. Among them was Pamela Lipkin, a well-known plastic surgeon. I telephoned and left a lengthy message on her office voice mail, explaining who I was and why I was calling. It was a shot in the dark, but she also had a reputation for being a social gadfly, so I thought that she might at least know of someone who had owned a starfish. Several weeks later she called back and when I answered the phone she started talking like we were old friends. It took me a few seconds to under-stand who was calling. "I had one," she blurted over the phone.

Lipkin is an intense and confident personality. When I asked her why she bought the starfish she told me it was an instinctive purchase. She had a "huge" collection of jewelry, she said, and she started collecting pieces by Suzanne Belperron in the 1970s. A pair of escargot earrings is one of her favorites. She was an early col-lector of JAR, the jeweler Joel Arthur Rosenthal, who has taken the world of fine jewelry by storm in recent years. She said that she owned a Boivin ruby and amethyst starfish for eight years, but "I never wore it," she said. It stayed mostly in her safe-deposit box. "I didn't have time to wear it. You kind of need a booster pack to wear it. It's heavy." She said that she bought it for herself and sold it at auction and believes it may be the same one that had turned up with a friend of hers. She swerved to add that a friend of hers in the midst of a messy divorce on Long Island had one but wouldn't talk about it. She was vague about which starfish was which. Then she offered to put me in touch with a friend of hers who currently owned a ruby and amethyst starfish. Nancy Marks.

I realized this was the name I had heard from Peter Edwards in London, the woman that his clients had seen wearing a starfish and were smitten with it. Nancy, the chairman of Ralph Rucci fashion designs at the time, was gracious and easy to talk with over the telephone. Some sense of pride over having such a beau-tiful piece was reflected in her voice.

When I asked her to tell me how she acquired the starfish, she began by explaining how her attitude toward collecting was changed radically by a theft ten years earlier. She and her husband, Howard Marks, chairman of an investment company, whose personal worth, according to *Forbes* magazine, is over a billion dollars, were burglarized in Los Angeles. "Everything was stolen. It was really traumatic, such an invasion of privacy," she explained, and the experience left her feeling that she didn't want any jewelry for a while. "It was just 'stuff.'" It took several years of neither thinking about jewelry nor wearing it before she rebounded and told her husband, "I don't want a ton of jewelry. I want ten fantastic pieces." When the two of them were in Paris in 2008 she saw a picture of a Boivin ruby and amethyst starfish brooch in the Christie's catalogue. "I knew nothing of its owners or history. I just admired it for its beauty. It was too big and too much, but Howard was going to bid on it anyway." The pair would be in flight leaving Paris during the actual auction. Midflight Nancy remembered that the auction was ongoing, and Howard told her that he had left a bid for it. Once they landed and checked the results, they were disappointed to learn that they had been outbid. Unbeknownst to his wife, Howard was determined to buy it for her and he set out to track down the starfish. I mentioned to her that it is very difficult, if not impossible, to get auction houses to reveal their buyers, but she assured me, "My husband can be very persuasive." He learned that the starfish had gone to New York to the Stephen Russell salon on Madison Avenue. It had sold for $369,410 at auction. For a hundred thousand more than the auction price, Howard bought the piece and managed to surprise her. "It was so weird. He just came in and said, 'Let's go for a walk. I need you to come with me,'" she remembered. When he presented her the leather case with the starfish in it, she was thrilled—if not wholly surprised.

I had already heard about the ripples it made when she wore it out to lunch in London. She and Howard are hardly celebrities, but they are a power couple when they step out in New York or London. She remembers wearing the starfish to a luncheon at the Museum of Modern Art in New York, also attended by the clothing designer Diane von Furstenberg. "Diane flipped out," Nancy said, laughing good-naturedly; she had enjoyed the admiration.

The starfish always attracted attention. It was somehow satisfying to know that the starfish was worn and not just kept under wraps, but Nancy echoed other owners when she told me that it is difficult to wear. It is best suited to be worn on a sturdy jacket or other stiff fabric. Its virtue lies in the way that its articulated limbs mold to the contour where it is pinned.

She invited me to her home to see it. It was one of those freezing New York winter days when the wind ripped along Central Park South where the Markses live in a penthouse atop the Ritz-Carlton Hotel. The elevator opened into the foyer of their apartment, an aerie furnished in cool neutral colors. Pieces of stone statuary accented the room. Nancy, a petite and pretty brunette with her hair pulled back simply in a bun and wearing scarce makeup, met me in a simple maroon sweater dress and wedge heels. She wore big gold hoop earrings but no other decorative jewelry. She guided me to the kitchen, where she made us tea and I looked down into the leafless trees in Central Park whose tops from this height looked like gray and brown lace. While the tea steeped Nancy disappeared momentarily and returned with a startling splash of color against the cool color palettes inside and out: her ruby and amethyst starfish brooch. She set it casually on the breakfast table between us.

I must have exhaled. This was the real deal. Her starfish with its long rays detailed by six cabochon rubies running down their spines looked just as I remembered the one I saw fleetingly at the Verdura party. It commanded the space between us. She offered it to me to handle. Its articulated gold fretwork and everything about it felt elegantly seamless. No point caught when I stroked it with my finger. I had heard enough jewelers talk about what made a Boivin starfish special that I knew what to look for. Tips of two rays were flipped at their ends to show their golden undersides, and it, like the one Millicent Rogers had owned, looked real enough to be a live creature. As we handled it, I noticed that a small amethyst was missing from its tiny setting hole. We talked for a moment of a jeweler who might be appropriate to make repairs and she showed me a fabulous gold cuff bracelet that she had asked him to make for her a few years back. It was obvious that she loved jewelry and chose her pieces discriminatingly. She was totally relaxed, rather than all atwitter, with their value and fineness. When she pinned it to the neckline of her burgundy dress, even light as flat as the winter light that morning caught in the perfectly rounded ruby at the center and radiated depth and warmth. I was always a little surprised at how, when a starfish is presented, after the surprise and a moment of admiration, there is really little else to say. There it was. It spoke for itself. Nancy turned her head so I could snap a photo of the starfish pinned to her dress. The focus quickly went to the piece, not the wearer. She smiled slightly, but all of our energy went toward the starfish, not each other.

We made small talk while we finished our tea and she told me a story about collecting fine jewelry. She had photographed the pieces that were stolen from her in Los Angeles ten years earlier. One was a diamond brooch created by JAR. It was reported to an organization called the Art Loss Register. When a friend saw the missing piece seven years later for sale in Hong Kong, the FBI was alerted and it was recovered shortly after being offered for sale by a New York jeweler. I was impressed to hear how this kind of recovery worked, and that it was possible to track down stolen jewelry. Later when I contacted the Art Loss Register the agent I spoke with told me a story that reminded me of Claudette Colbert's story of putting down her Pan Am bag with her starfish in it and finding it gone when she remembered to take it with her. In 2006 the young Duchess of Argyll set down her hand luggage at the Glasgow Airport. A three-string pearl necklace, a Cartier brooch, a large emerald ring, and a pair of pearl earrings were packed inside. The duchess realized the bag was missing before she even began the car trip back to Inveraray Castle. She reported the theft to the airport police at the Art Loss Register. Six years later she spotted her Cartier brooch being offered for sale at the Edinburgh auction house Lyon & Turnbull, and enlisted the Art Loss Register's help. Further investigations revealed a Glasgow dealer had purchased all four pieces at the "Unclaimed Property" department from the British Airports Association. One may wonder if the duchess had bothered to follow up on her claim, but maybe duchesses don't do that. Of course, she was overjoyed to have some of her jewelry back, especially the brooch of diamonds and sapphires that Cartier had made for her grandmother. Her square-cut diamond ring and a pair of pearl earrings surrounded by tourmalines and diamonds were still missing. Besides being a good tale, the story was a reminder of what a commodity jewelry is. The agent whom I spoke with at the Art Loss Register told me that he had never had a starfish reported missing.

Nancy Marks clearly was attracted to the starfish purely for its beauty, but to many people it was primarily an economic good whose value fluctuated with the market. I wanted to think that her starfish was Claudette Colbert's, resurfaced after all these years, but there was no certainty. It was definitely not Millicent Rogers's with its baguette amethysts circling the central ruby.

During the elevator ride down to the ground floor I thought back to the Markses' apartment and Nancy's stewardship of the starfish. It was a place where a Boivin ruby and amethyst starfish belonged, the kind of rarefied and quietly elegant rooms away from the bustle of life below where I had imagined they would wash up.

And then I had a stroke of unexpected good luck. I found a source who knew who owned one of the original Boivin starfish, probably the Millicent Rogers one, but wouldn't tell me. I had developed this source in the process of running down the woman Lee Siegelson had seen wearing it, and after Nicholas Luchsinger's remark that it belonged to an American in New York. I decided to name her/him Deep Throat in honor of the secret source who coached the reporters Woodward and Bernstein in their investigation of the Watergate scandal. Their Deep Throat gave them hints. My Deep Throat told me that the owner had an important position in the music world, and had jewelry from "all the masters," which could include Cartier, Tiffany, Van Cleef & Arpels, Boucheron, and Belperron. The owner was a Van Cleef client, Deep Throat said, which I already surmised.

So now I was closing in on my little school of starfish. I knew where two were. Susan Rotenstreich had hers on Park Avenue in New York and Nancy Marks's was on Central Park South. If Deep Throat knew what he/she was talking about, it sounded like a third was also a stone's throw away from the two owners I knew of in New York. I remained hopeful that I could find the third. I had always known there would be some unsolved mysteries in the starfish story and that I would probably not be able to draw a neat line to all the people who had owned each starfish since their creation. I had even thought when I left Paris that I just might have to accept that I could not discover who owned Millicent Rogers's starfish today. But as my hunt continued, and now that I had located two, the mystery of the Millicent Rogers starfish ate at me. After all, I was her biographer and hers was the starfish that I had followed down the rabbit hole into this whole dazzling and sometimes daunting world after the Verdura party. I promised myself I would find it.

Chapter Nineteen

M Y HUSBAND AND I USED TO DO A LITTLE SCUBA
diving. I remember how easy it was to become dis-
oriented underwater. At this point in my search, I
had a similar feeling hunting for the starfish. It
was hard to know which way to turn. There were definitely more
than the three I originally believed existed, but there were also
obviously different classes, different grades. Not all were on
the level of the first few masterpieces turned out by Boivin. I had
learned that the jewelry world abhorred the idea of identifying
later versions as reproductions. The interests of the jewelers were
best served by the idea that they were all more or less the same, with
the later versions basking in the price effect created by the early
wonderful versions. Confusion reigns, and it isn't all accidental. I
had to keep Susan Abeles's admonition about wolves in mind.

More like sharks, I was thinking, swimming among the starfish. How many more have been made beyond the three to five Boivin originals? I guessed there were a half-dozen reproductions out there, maybe more. I had seen one at Christie's. Maybe Pamela Lipkin's Long Island friend had one. Another had sold from Christie's, and I had to assume there could be a few more that had evaded notice if they had not crossed the well-worn paths of New York, London, and Paris jewelers. It definitely seemed there were more than the three ruby and amethyst Boivin starfish that had been mentioned in Christie's auction catalogue notes. The standards for authenticity in fine jewelry were a bit different than they might be for, say, modern paintings, and they diluted the market created by the original works of art.

For instance: Christie's auction records showed five starfish sales since 1996. One that had sold in 2010 in Switzerland for $184,278 was dated as being from the 1960s and was said to measure 12.2 centimeters in diameter, a centimeter larger than the originals. It appeared to be the same piece that had been offered at Christie's in New York in 2006 with the information that it had been the property of Oscar de la Renta. Its lot description at that time followed the notes that accompanied the originals and said that it was dated circa 1935. Yet a salesroom notice on the same page advised, "Please note that the starfish is a recent example and was most likely manufactured in the 1980s." For whatever reasons, that starfish didn't sell.

One of the starfish that had passed through Christie's auctions in the last twenty years was unaccounted for. It had sold in 2006 and it wasn't the one that Susan Rotenstreich or Nancy Marks had. It wasn't the Oscar de la Renta one and it wasn't Millicent Rogers's. I was determined to find it, but I was out of ideas about where to look. A jeweler in London had told me about a woman who frequented auctions in Paris and Geneva who often took her dog, a standard poodle, with her to the sales. The mystery woman wore a flamingo brooch that was made by Cartier. It was the brooch, copied from an original that had belonged to the Duchess of Windsor, that had stuck in my acquaintance's mind rather than her name. The only clue she could give me was that the woman, a known collector who sat in the same row at auctions as the leading French dealers, "who huddle together and behave like naughty schoolchildren at the back of the class," was on good terms with the Landrigans at Verdura. It seemed so little to go on, but by now I had great respect for how small the jewelry world was. I asked Ward Landrigan if he knew of a woman who fit this description. A message promptly came back from his assistant, Betty Kojik, that it was Suzanne Tennenbaum, a collector who lived in Los Angeles. Betty had contacted her on my behalf and Tennenbaum agreed to speak with me. Her e-mail address was included. The hint sent me in a new direction, for which I was hugely grateful.

Tennenbaum knew all about the starfish, but she said that she had never owned one. She had seen a few at auction that she suspected were the later ones that Asprey made when they revived the designs in the eighties and nineties. Those sounded like the ones that Murray Mondschein sold at Fred Leighton. "There are probably only a couple of them that are actually old and one of them sold in Paris probably five years ago . . . I know a dealer bought that one," she told me. She remembered that thirty years ago there had been two older starfish, both a ruby and amethyst one and an emerald and aquamarine version, in a store on Rue Saint-Honoré in Paris that sounded like Michel Perinet's. I jumped to the conclusion that the first one she mentioned might have been the third original that was kept by Boivin. The emerald and aquamarine starfish that was in his store had been used on the cover of the first book, *Le Prix des Bijoux,* by Françoise Cailles, an illustrated review of international jewelry auctions written in 1986. At last I was able to recognize and identify some of the signposts on the starfish's trails. Tennenbaum also recalled seeing a ruby and amethyst starfish in the early 1990s at an auction in Saint Moritz. "Probably someone like Fred Leighton bought it and it is one of the five circulating around now," she commented. It interested me that she was speaking of five starfish. And I always perked up when Murray was mentioned. Tennenbaum suspected that the one she saw was one of the later ones. "They are completely unwearable," in her opinion.

Her interest in jewelry, she explained, was mostly personal but she worked as a dealer on the side. She also voiced the same lament that I was hearing from vintage jewelry fanciers and dealers everywhere. "Prices are out of control in my opinion. Everything is overpriced." She knew that Nathalie Hocq, who had bought the Boivin brand, had made a few "cheaper ones" with Frédéric Chambre, an auctioneer and jewelry personality who worked with the Pierre Bergé auction house in Paris. Starfish, as a species, seemed to abound. But the magnificent three, four, or five first produced by Boivin were scattered and elusive.

"The newer ones have diluted the market a bit," Tennenbaum added. This seems to be what Ralph Esmerian feared when he first saw an—ahem—reproduction. Tennenbaum spoke knowledgeably about record books of the type that Hocq and others hold on to so tightly. She mistrusted them. "There are no drawings in those books. People can put in what they want."

The Boivin archives were a hole in my story. When Madame Boivin's daughter and heir to the business, Germaine, turned sixty-six in 1964 she began to think of a future without the Boivin business and she took on a new assistant, Jacques Bernard. According to Françoise Cailles in her book about Boivin, Bernard was an accomplished jeweler, though I would be told by another jeweler that he was more of a businessman than a creative designer. There was a hazy tale of financial and marital intrigue in that account, as well, but I could not verify it.

I was also hearing that the Boivin brand percolates on the back burner of another wealthy, attractive, interesting woman. A Swiss-French beauty—and by repute a formidable personality—Nathalie Hocq owns the Boivin brand and the sketches, books, personal recollections, and archives that go along with it. These are the papers that Françoise Cailles consults to authenticate pieces of Boivin jewelry when she is hired to do so and they are mostly what made up the basis for her book *René Boivin: Jeweller*. Yet she never shows her copies of the archives to anyone.

Nathalie Hocq (her married last name is Choay) is yet another colorful if vexing player in the Boivin story. She is part of the royalty of the European jewelry world. Her father, former president of Cartier, insisted that she get a degree in economics, study marketing, and understand finance. In 1972 when she was twenty-one, he appointed her marketing director of Cartier. She rose quickly and was known for being elusive even then. An exotically pretty, stylish, and fragile-looking woman in her photographs, she smoked big man-sized cigars from a sandalwood humidor on her desk. At twenty-five she had risen to become the jewelry director of Cartier's multimillion-dollar operation in ninety countries. I wanted to meet her and hoped that there was information about the starfish in the archives. But she never responded to my e-mail messages, letters, or phone calls.

Owning the Boivin archives gives Hocq the license to reproduce the Boivin designs, including the starfish. She partnered in one reported instance to do so with Pierre Bergé, the eighty-four-year-old multimillionaire French businessman who was a partner of the late couturier Yves Saint Laurent in life and business. The Pierre Bergé auction house (PBA) is one of his properties, and in 2012 a contemporary starfish credited as a Boivin sold at PBA for €42,000. Without a Boivin store in existence, auctions are the standard method for introducing such reproductions to the market. New York jewelry designer and socialite Ann Ziff remembered seeing a Boivin starfish at the Pierre Bergé auction house in Paris. PBA included an image from the Boivin archive to promote the starfish for sale, a drawing bearing the official circular stamp from René Boivin that one jeweler explained to me was proof that the design came from the Boivin archives belonging to Nathalie Hocq. Determined to avoid any exposure, Pierre Bergé's *chargée* of communications nevertheless assured me that Pierre knew "nothing about the Boivin starfish." I chalked this up to a term I'd confected to describe such conversations: "jeweler speak." She obfuscated further by adding that Frédéric Chambre, who used to work at PBA, was the only one who knew about Boivin. Could she put me in touch with him? I asked. "Unfortunately not," was her reply. The French were *formidable* when they closed ranks. The fact that Hocq had permitted and, it seemed, partnered to make a few new starfish and offered them at auction remained.

Now in her sixties, Hocq is a *grande dame* of the international jewelry world. The one time that I reached her on her cell phone she explained that she was driving in traffic but would call me back. My call was never returned, and my letters, sent to her home in Geneva, were returned, unopened. She obviously was not going to discuss Boivin. Some colleagues believe that she is undecided about what to do with the archives. Yet that stamped image of the starfish from Bergé is public record of her attempt to re-create the design in at least one instance. Another guess about reasons for her reticence is that the Boivin archives are extensive and in disarray. Sometimes I wondered if they existed at all, but Sam Loxton assured me they did. He knew someone who had worked "on the bench" for Asprey who had crated and moved the archives between London and Geneva, Hocq's city of residence. Unlike Olivier Baroin's meticulous digitalization of Belperron's records and archives that permit him to look up anything with a touch of his computer keyboard, the Boivin archive is not available to be referenced. I wondered if it might not have a record of sale for the third starfish and a few other details. However, as Evelyne Possémé at the Musée des Arts Décoratifs consoled me, "It may well have been in code anyway."

At the beginning of my search I would have thought it ridiculous that the seventy-five-year-old archives of a defunct jewelry house and the names of long-dead original clients would be guarded like the Hope diamond. But then I didn't know how dodgy the jewelry business is. Jewelers, I have to admit, have a penchant for drama, and secrecy is par for the course.

I was about to give up on finding the other starfish when I received an e-mail from a West Coast jewelry dealer.

> Hello Cherie,
>
> Suzanne Tennenbaum sent your email to me, my name is Ann Marie Stanton and I'm a jewelry dealer in Beverly Hills. It was my pleasure to sell one of the magnificent Boivin starfish about six years ago to a woman who wears her jewelry and loves it.
>
> I would be happy to help you in any way possible and I'm sure my client would also.
>
> Best,
>
> Ann Marie

Her message seemed almost too good to be true, promising access both to her and the starfish's owner. I quickly learned that she had acquired what appeared to be the last original Boivin starfish, the one the house of Boivin had evidently held close for decades, for the television and movie actress Jennifer Tilly. "Jennifer is intrigued with jewelry and she is a very sophisticated collector," Stanton explained to me. Better yet, Jennifer was willing to talk about it.

Ann Marie Stanton worked for herself buying and selling

antique and estate jewelry in Beverly Hills. She told me that she
first became aware of the Boivin ruby and amethyst starfish when
one came up for sale from Christie's in Geneva in 2006. That was
the one that I believed had passed through Lee Siegelson's hands,
described by Janet Zapata in the written account of her research
about it for Lee Siegelson as the third starfish. She stated that it
had stayed "in the family of the original purchasers until now."
Lee Siegelson and his assistant Sarah Davis would tell me only
that the former owner had been in Europe, not the United States.
Ann Marie had only seen images of it in the catalogue when she
took note of it.

I jumped to the conclusion that it must have been the later
Oscar de la Renta brooch, but in fact the auction notes for the de
la Renta one explained, "A similar brooch was sold in Christie's
Geneva, on May 17, 2006, lot 381 for $293,000." The de la Renta
one at Christie's Geneva was sold, according to the catalogue, in
2010 for CHF 184,000.[1,2] Its price was the best indicator that it
was not an original.

Ann Marie was a refreshing change from the French and New
York dealers who got jittery discussing their clients. Her client,
Jennifer Tilly, was the dream owner of a Boivin brooch from my
point of view. Tilly, who has appeared in over sixty films during
her acting career and was nominated for an Oscar for her role in
Bullets over Broadway, may be best known to audiences today as a
gambler on the World Series of Poker. She talked openly about
her passion for jewelry and her pride in her collection. "She wears
it," Stanton told me flatly. Jennifer's pieces aren't sitting around,
hidden in a vault.

Tilly's profile as a movie actress and professional gambler is
more public to begin with than those of the society figures who
own starfish, and it is one reason she is more comfortable talking
about her jewelry. "I always really loved jewelry. I used to watch
Joan Rivers ask the stars on the red carpet whose pieces they were

wearing. When someone said, 'It's mine,' that was the person I wanted to be," Tilly said in her distinctively high, raspy voice. She chronicled her evolution as a collector. "In the past I loved the kitschy stuff that looked like a great-aunt in Palm Beach had left it to you. Those coral and turquoise animals." She laughed. "Then I got more serious."

Serious meant recognizing the brands and paying higher prices. JAR. Boivin. Belperron. "You can buy a diamond, a big emerald. Those are easy, but it's the art pieces that interest me," explained Tilly, remembering how Joan Crawford wore her charm bracelet with Oscars and love-note charms dangling from it. "I loved it," enthused Jennifer, who looks down a little on the trend of actresses wearing borrowed dresses and borrowed jewelry rather than reflecting their taste by wearing their own. She bought herself a fabled Bulgari brooch in the 2011 estate sale of Liz Taylor. "It was the brooch that Eddie Fisher gave her when she was in Rome making *Cleopatra*. She ran off with Burton, so he sent her the bill and she paid for it!" Tilly told me, thrilled. "There is a lot of beauty in jewels and the stories behind them," she said, and added with pride, "I buy my own jewelry. I buy my taste and what appeals to me. That's it. I have friends who get pieces from their husbands and they say, 'Oh, I wish he'd asked my opinion.' Then you get something you don't love but you have to wear it so he'll buy you a present again." That was not her problem. This reminded me of what Ward Landrigan had said about the changed nature of the jewelry business in recent years. "Women buy jewelry for themselves now. In the past, women used to wait for a guy to buy something. And very often, if he bought something he would buy the wrong thing!"

The *right* jewelry, in her opinion, matters. "It is how you project yourself. I love the golden age when Joan Crawford and Marlene Dietrich owned their own jewelry or it was passed down from one

generation to the next. Today it is a more disposable culture."
Jennifer Tilly joins the ranks of other professional or wealthy
women like Colbert, Rogers, or Dr. Pamela Lipkin, who have
bought their own starfish. Nancy Marks, Claudia Cohen, and
Susan Rotenstreich were aided by prosperous husbands, but they,
too, have professional identities. Tilly proudly wears three JAR
brooches at a time. She also has a gold Boivin cow skull that was
exhibited in the Victoria and Albert Museum. "You'll never see
that again. Belperron is dead. Boivin is dead. They can't be
churning out new pieces." That's one reason jewelry by distinctive quality designers is steadily increasing in value.

Just as Ann Marie Stanton had told me, Tilly wears her starfish, like her other large brooches, on black dresses. "They are a
great frame for the brooches. A 1930s silk gown would be okay.
Or a simple black dress, tea length. No jeans!" Tilly laughed.

Scale, color, and design are what attracted her to the starfish.
"I loved this starfish from the beginning," she said. She had seen
the photo of Millicent Rogers with her starfish on her shoulder,
even though the starfish being touted for sale was not Rogers's.
The iconic Richard Rutledge photo of Rogers wearing it is part
of the legend of the piece and what the auctioneer at Christie's used
to promote it. "It was so big and bold and I really wanted it. I
thought it was incredibly chic and the colors were muted," she concluded after seeing the catalogue in color. It inspired her to leave
a bid on it, but as she has become a more experienced collector
she prefers being on the phone or having someone else do her bidding.

A year and a half later Christie's advertised the Oscar de la
Renta starfish, but when Tilly learned that it wasn't one of the
original ones, she didn't bid. "You just have to wait," she concluded. It took discipline. Ann Marie Stanton became her partner in shopping for a starfish. In a prime example of the jewelry

world network, it was Susan Abeles, whom I had met at the
Bonhams auction house in New York and who used to work for
Lee Siegelson, who spoke to someone at Doyle, where she also
used to work (with Berj Zavian), who knew Ann Marie's West
Coast partner, Nan. Nan told Ann Marie a starfish was available.
When Stanton heard about it she asked the owner to send her
photos of it. Jennifer knew she wanted the starfish, but Stanton
wanted to negotiate the price if she could. Lee Siegelson in New
York sent the piece through Brink's insured shipping service for
Stanton and Tilly to look at. Tilly remembers the day it arrived
in Stanton's Beverly Hills office. "When they pulled it out of the
box, it was beautiful!" She was smitten by it. "I knew I would put
it on a payment plan. I wanted it." Tilly said that this kind of fine
vintage jewelry "costs a lot." It's not like buying a designer dress
or handbag, so she considered it to be an investment worth putting on a payment plan if she couldn't afford it outright. She
regarded it as a commodity. "I'm not going to sell, but I could
during hard times if I needed to." Stanton negotiated a price with
Lee Siegelson, but the sticking point was the payment plan Tilly
needed to purchase it. Lee finally acquiesced to payments spread
out over several months. The starfish would stay with Stanton
until it was paid for. It was an old-fashioned "layaway plan" fi-
nanced with a loan. The purchase price was around four hundred
thousand dollars, which all parties, except one who slipped, told
me they couldn't exactly remember seven years later.

Meanwhile, Tilly enjoys her jewelry and is unapologetic about
wearing big expensive pieces. She has worn her starfish nine or ten
times. She does not hide it away in a safe or bank vault. "If I had
pieces in the vault I would never end up wearing them. Jewelry is
to wear," she asserted, and said that she often thought of the photo
of Millicent Rogers wearing her starfish. "She wore her jewelry
every day to express herself. When I wear mine it makes me happy

and other people, too. It just makes the day a little brighter. The starfish is a great conversation piece. People want to know about jewelry like this," she said.

Tilly added that she did not wear her starfish to play poker because "it is too elegant. I have to look like a lady gambler on television." She is known for her voluptuous figure and the deep cleavage she has revealed at the poker table, but perhaps the starfish would be a further distraction to her opponents. With her physical stature and profile she can pull off wearing the large brooch. It amuses her that she is the second Hollywood actress (that we know of) to own one.

I surmised that Tilly's starfish was bought by Stephen Russell at auction in Geneva. I was beginning to get the idea that, despite their laid-back personas, Stephen Feuerman and Russell Zelentz were the bloodhounds of the starfish market, always on alert for the appearance of one. The price of a ruby and amethyst Boivin starfish had tripled since Susan Rotenstreich's husband bought hers in 1996. Despite its estimate of $54,000 to $66,000, Russell paid $287,055 in Geneva. Lee Siegelson was his partner, and Stanton tells me she negotiated a price with Lee. More intriguing to me was Christie's catalogue note for the piece that claimed it was bought *directly from Boivin* and was the third model of the starfish. I take this to mean that it is the one that followed Colbert's and Rogers's off the drawing board in Paris. The bit worth pondering was "bought directly from Boivin." By 2006, Boivin's doors had been closed for more than twenty years. I recalled an image from the book *Modern Jewelry: An International Survey 1890–1963* by Graham Hughes that accompanied the 1963 exhibition at the Victoria and Albert Museum in London. It included a photo of this starfish. Boivin was listed in the owner's column. Was it possible that the Boivin family had kept the starfish until 2006? Or that Françoise Cailles, as authenticator, had owned it? Of course, any number of owners could have bought directly from Boivin in the 1930s and kept their starfish in the family for seventy-eight years. Janet Zapata's notes on the starfish asserted that it had "remained in the family of the original purchasers until now." It was probably as close as I was going to get to the truth unless Cailles would break her silence.

The starfish in the photo in the Graham Hughes book was grouped with three other Boivin creations, including Juliette Moutard's famous chameleon brooch that allows the wearer to change the torso's colors by rotating the body when you press the chameleon's tongue. It still strikes me as so magically ingenious, making fine jewelry into a toy! Emmanuelle Chassard in Paris explained this kind of fun as the beauty of Boivin. A woman who went to a party displayed her chameleon in one color at the beginning of the evening and changed it to a different color later. (Interestingly enough, this chameleon has been lost and subsequently found twice.) I had to admit that fashionable rich women seemed to have a larger sense of play and whimsy in 1930s Paris than I felt they did today. The book with images of the chameleon and starfish listed the designer and owner alongside each piece and the starfish in the photo was said to be owned by Boivin. It is tough to make out in the photo, but that starfish appeared to have rays two and five flipped on the ends, as does the one pictured for sale from Christie's in 2006. It also looks like the same starfish that was shown larger than its actual size and in full four-color glory in the book *René Boivin: Jeweller,* which Françoise Cailles wrote for Boivin in 1994. It all seems to add up that this is the starfish, "the superb starfish" as Christie's called it, the third, that has ended up with Jennifer Tilly. I liked to think of it traveling on her ample bosom, making the rounds in Hollywood.

Some months later, I met Ann Marie Stanton at the Original Miami Beach jewelry show and she encouraged me to come have

a look for myself at Jennifer's starfish. I went to L.A. to see it.
Jennifer was out of town at the time, but Ann Marie had brought
it into her mirrored fourth-floor office, hardly bigger than a
closet, in the Wells Fargo Building in Beverly Hills. Her ten-year-
old dog, half poodle, half schnauzer, named Charlie, lay curled
in his doghouse, a black-and-white tepee, on the floor next to us.
Ann Marie, animated and good-natured, rather ceremoniously got
into her safe and removed the gray stationery-note-sized box with
a color photocopy of a photo of the starfish on the top. When she
opened it, the "superb" starfish was nestled into the foam in a
space cut out for its shape. I imagined that this starfish was the last
one I was likely to see for myself so I decided to savor the moment.
It was by all standards a beautiful example of why the starfish is so
captivating. In the late morning light in Ann Marie's office, its reds
and purples danced. As I picked it up, its articulated rays quaked
and spread with the movement of my hands. "Would you like to
try it on?" asked Ann Marie. Yes, I said. Yes. I pinned it onto my
left shoulder and admired it in the floor-to-ceiling mirrors.

Ann Marie and I, with Charlie at our feet, ducked out for a
quick lunch and recapped a few things about the starfish. She explained to me that she was new to the jewelry business, unlike
many of the fifth- and sixth-generation jewelers that dominate it.
"That's why it is an old-world business. You can walk out of an
office with a bag of jewelry worth millions on your signature if
everyone knows your family and who you are," she explained. As
for the Boivin starfish, "These pieces self-select. There aren't that
many people who have the funds and you have to have confidence
to wear them. And there are only so many of them." I told her
that counting Jennifer's I knew of four. We discussed some of the
later reproductions, which she calls "reissued starfish." With the
pride of an adoption agent who has made a good match, she says
that she considers Jennifer and the starfish a fitting combination.
"Jennifer gambles. Jewelry is a gamble, too."

Back in Stanton's office I took the starfish out of its box again and held it in my palm. Then I took a long, lingering last look at it and handed it back to her. It had been almost five years since the first starfish bewitched me at Verdura. I did not know if I would hold one again.

Chapter Twenty

LEAVING LOS ANGELES, I TOOK STOCK OF WHERE I WAS IN MY starfish hunt. I had verified the existence of four original starfish:

1. Nancy Marks's thoroughbred beauty, purchased at auction in Paris. It might be Claudette Colbert's missing version, back through some mysterious process, from years in the outer darkness.

2. Susan Rotenstreich's slightly smaller piece. An original Moutard version, which seemed to have crept into the lineup with the three (or four?) larger brooches. An alternate thought: who is to say that this smaller starfish wasn't the first one that Claudette bought that reemerged with Joanne Cummings and then sold to Susan? It seemed unlikely, but possible.

3. Jennifer Tilly's, bought from Lee Siegelson, who

acquired it in Geneva. Very possibly the one that was held back by Boivin or some other "original owner" until 2006.

4.   Millicent Rogers's version with the amethyst baguettes that differentiate it from the others. I had traced it from her daughter-in-law Jackie to Henry Baker to Sam Loxton, to Lee Siegelson, and then to a client of Van Cleef & Arpels whom I could not identify.

To complicate matters further, because I could not trace the provenances all the way, it is possible that Nancy Marks's model is the one held back by Boivin and Jennifer Tilly owned the piece first bought by Claudette Colbert.

This was all a snapshot, the best I could do from everything I knew currently. I had to admit, though, that there were previous appearances of starfish that just didn't fit into the trail of ownership I had puzzled out. The biggest irritation for me was that Millicent's version, which had gotten me into this whole exercise, and was the only one I could trace with certainty from its birth, had slipped away into unknown hands in the last few years. I didn't know where it was. I only had a hint from Van Cleef in Paris that its owner lived in New York.

It was not a neat picture. There were unresolved tips, brief glimpses that didn't fit into my list of four. I had to think there might be another one out there. Did the friend of Pamela Lipkin's who was in the midst of a divorce actually own an original? And I was beginning to accept that I would probably never know which of the starfish had been Claudette Colbert's. I wasn't even sure that Boivin's archives and sales records could help solve that mystery. The missing brooch had somehow been thrown back into the sea of jewelers and collectors when it resurfaced from the dark side. Unsurprisingly, it traveled without provenance. It seemed pretty obvious that one of the starfish in circulation had been Colbert's, but none of the jewelers I talked to would hazard a guess about which one it was.

I had heard the story of a starfish that I thought could have been Claudette Colbert's, emerging to a new life in Paris in the 1980s. The legendary late socialite São Schlumberger, married to the aristocratic French oil drilling tycoon Pierre Schlumberger, had once owned one. She fit the profile of the kind of woman who had a Boivin starfish. Wildly extravagant right up to her death in 2007, the Portuguese-born beauty lived a French fairy-tale life in a five-story eighteenth-century mansion, in Paris. It was filled with Rothkos, Lichtensteins, and all manner of fine art. Andy Warhol did a silkscreen portrait of São, heightening her legend. Salvador Dalí painted her, too. She gave parties for fifteen hundred guests, wore haute couture, and turned up once at Studio 54 in New York wearing major diamonds and rubies from Van Cleef & Arpels. She loved jewelry. Her husband gave her a fifty-one-carat Golconda diamond ring in a brown paper bag. Everything about her was excessive, including her public affair with the Egyptian prince Naguib Abdallah, whom her husband supported to keep her happy.

Ralph Esmerian had mentioned to me in a letter that New York jewelry designer Christopher Walling, whose innovative designs have been worn by a host of celebrities and society figures, including Queen Noor, Danielle Steel, and Liz Taylor, told him that São had a Boivin ruby and amethyst starfish.

A great raconteur, Walling recalled to me being with São when she asked her husband Pierre which of her many diamonds she should wear to a dinner with the Queen of England. Pierre responed, "All of them! If not now, when?" To criticism that it was vulgar to wear so much jewelry, São also memorably retorted, "It's only vulgar if you don't have it." Walling, a tall, dapper moustachioed man in cowboy boots and a camel's hair jacket, smiled, eyes twinkling like the gemstones he set in his jewelry designs, as he told me the story. He remembered that São was wearing her

ruby and amethyst starfish brooch when he accompanied her to
one of fashion arbiter Eleanor Lambert's shows. Lambert was the
creator of the International Best Dressed List. Walling explained
that São did not wear her Boivin starfish to fancy dress balls, like
those at Versailles, where she arrived in a maroon Rolls-Royce and
was more likely to have on a ruby and diamond necklace that had
belonged to Marie Antoinette. While the starfish was beautiful,
it wasn't fine or fancy enough for formal royal occasions. He does
not know what became of her starfish after her death, but it may
well be tied up in the rancorous relationship that she had with
her daughter, Victoire. I started conjuring the possibilities. Could
São's have been the one that turned up for sale in 2012 at Emmanuelle Chassard's La Galerie Parisienne in Paris? Or could it have
been Claudette Colbert's? Walling produced a photograph of a
smiling São with her starfish pinned to the left shoulder of her
fur coat as she and Walling headed out to a party for the gemstone artist Andreas von Zadora-Gerlof at Malcolm Forbes's in
1992. In the photograph, apparently taken with a flash, the color
of the stones in the starfish is somewhat washed out and I would
have mistaken them for sapphires or aquamarines, but Walling is
clear. They were rubies and amethysts. With a magnifying glass I
tried to see which rays were flipped. The fourth was obviously
curled up, but I could not see the top of the ray on her shoulder.
As I studied the image of the starfish that Chassard sent to me
saying it had sold "recently," I saw that it had the first and fourth
rays turned up at their ends. This is hardly conclusive, but it does
suggest that the starfish she sold, for whatever reason, could have
been São's. She died in 2007. Alain, Emmanuelle Chassard's father,
offered another clue when he told me in Miami, the following year,
that the starfish that went through the Chassard store was from a
special old family, and a special piece. The Schlumbergers' would
meet his description. Emmanuelle had figured prominently in a
New York Times story in 2010 about Boivin. She talked about Boivin's

innovative designs and, case in point, a jewelry sale at Christie's in Geneva a month earlier that included a Boivin starfish, "a mythical piece of which no more than 4 or 5 were ever made," but when I went back to the auction sale record, that starfish was a larger and later version. A reproduction. It was impossible to know whether it or another had been the one sold from La Galerie Parisienne a year later. Or whether it could have been São's. Of course, I had asked, but Chassard wouldn't tell me.

During our interview a light went on in Christopher Walling's head and he brightened as he said, "I think I know who has Rogers's now. At least I can make an educated guess." Without giving away the name that had come to mind, he promised to check out his hunch and get back to me. A few days later, he told me that Ann Ziff had two starfish. He thought he remembered seeing her with one when they flew together in her G5 aircraft some years back. This news gave me a fresh shot of adrenaline. Ziff was a well-known jewelry fancier, she now designed jewelry herself, and she was a recognized patron of the arts. The only doubt I harbored was Nicholas Luchsinger's assertion when I interviewed him at Van Cleef in Paris that the client who had the Rogers starfish was "very, very private." Ziff was not that private, but I still hoped. My excitement was short-lived. I wrote to Deep Throat, who had told me that while he/she could not tell me outright who owned the Rogers starfish, he/she would confirm it for me only when I discovered it on my own. The answer came back promptly. "No!" I explained I had heard that Ziff had two. "Ask her to show it to you," was the only riposte.

Walling continued to think that one of Ziff's starfish might be Millicent Rogers's. I asked him why he thought someone would want two. The answer was obvious to him. He put his hand to his waist. Two would make a fabulous belt buckle, he explained. Oh. And here I had been straining in my fantasies to figure out how I might wear *one* starfish the size of my hand. So pedestrian. I recalled that Millicent's son Arturo thought he remembered that a second starfish had shown up for his mother to consider when they lived on their estate in Virginia during World War II. Millicent had also seen the appeal of wearing two, fashioning them into a belt buckle, yet in the end she did not keep the second starfish.

Several months later, I spoke with Ann Ziff. She had had two starfish, but only one was ruby and amethyst. Ziff fit several of the categories Deep Throat had outlined for me in his/her clues to the owner of the Millicent Rogers brooch. She was deeply involved in the musical arts. Her mother had been a famous opera singer and Ziff herself had been chair of the Metropolitan Opera in New York. She also, in her present configuration and encouraged by her late husband, the magazine publishing magnate William Ziff Jr., designed her own jewelry and was the principal in Tamsen Z, a fine jewelry store on Madison Avenue in New York. She was extremely easy to speak with and forthcoming about her jewelry.

"I first saw a starfish in the 1980s," she told me. Echoing Lee Siegelson's inability to recall the woman who was wearing the piece, but distinctly remembering the sight of the starfish, Ann said unabashedly, "I loved it. I didn't care who had it. I just thought to myself, *there's one*. I didn't ask her about it, but I kept an eye out." When one showed up for sale at auction through Sotheby's in Geneva in 1991, she bought it.

Ziff had an early appreciation for Boivin. The starfish was among a Boivin lobster, a "salamander with a click tail," and a ring with bangles that she and her husband William flew to Geneva to bid on. She remembered, "We bought probably fifteen to twenty-seven pieces." All Boivin. The starfish was among them and she says that she did not know whose collection they had come from.

There were also several small tiger's eye and citrine starfish in her collection, but she said that she wore her ruby and amethyst Boivin starfish "all the time. It was perfect on a suit jacket. I just put it on the shoulder pad." Somewhat hostage to etiquette, Ziff said she felt correct wearing the starfish during the day because it was made of colored gems. It used to be, "you didn't wear diamonds during the day," she explained. But she also wore her starfish at night on an off-the-shoulder pleated evening dress made of heavy black satin. When she owned both an emerald and aquamarine starfish, and a ruby and amethyst one, she wore them together. "The green one on one side, the red one on the other," she explained. And she wore the ruby and amethyst starfish at her waist on an evening gown.

The Boivin pieces appealed to her aesthetic and jewelry-making senses. "The appeal of those pieces is the engineering. Now jewelers don't study and know how to do that. It's too labor intensive. That tippy end on the starfish tentacle. You touch it and the whole thing moves." She spoke with childish glee over the marvel of the starfish. "They are works of art," she concluded. In fact, Ziff's "salamander with a click tail" turned out to be a chameleon with a click tongue, but the pleasure of making it change colors is the same no matter the anatomy involved. "When you wear it, people see it change from ruby to green. It's fun."

Ziff loaned her aquamarine and emerald Boivin starfish to soprano Renée Fleming to wear for her performance of Cesar Franck's *Panis Angelicus* at the Mainz Cathedral in Germany in 2005. It shone resplendently on her low-cut off-the-shoulder brown-and-beige-colored taffeta gown. The image of her wearing it was broadcast this year when she was designated a musical treasure by the Library of Congress. Though Fleming's rich voice rises above any competition, the starfish, moving with her breath and trills, did, however, distract the viewer.

Ziff sold her starfish in 2014, four years after she opened Tamsen Z and started making jewelry of her own. "People always asked me if I made what I was wearing," she said. She wanted to emphasize her own designs at the time. So in 2014 she sold both her ruby and amethyst and emerald and aquamarine starfish through Christie's in New York. She now speaks in the past tense about being a starfish owner, and she said she does not know who bought hers. She kept it for twenty-three years, and even though hers has moved on in the world, she still admires a starfish when she sees one, as she did "five or eight years ago on a Met board member." She cannot recall who it was and she suspects "it was more modern." Such sightings seem rare even among the women who have had Boivin starfish. This caused my antennae to twitch a little. It had been only four years since the Rogers starfish had sold, so I had to assume that the starfish she had seen could not have been Rogers's. Uncertain about the sales dates and location of the starfish when we spoke, she promised to have her office provide them to me later.

Serendipity played its part in my starfish hunt. I was experiencing a lull in my starfish discovery during a July spent in Nantucket when I jumped out of a boat into the harbor on a steamy hot day. When I came to the surface my friends noticed that I was wearing only one pearl earring. Several days later I went shopping to replace it and ended up at a store called Water Jewels on Center Street. Its British owner, Barbara Harris, lectured me sternly for swimming with pearls. She could not help me replace a single earring, but as we talked I said that I was writing about some jewelry and mentioned Boivin. I was trying to prove to her that I wasn't a total fool, even if I had gone swimming in my good pearl earrings. She immediately came to life. Barbara knew a lot about Boivin and the starfish brooches. She had seen one in Paris thirty years earlier when she was a design student. I went back to her shop the following day to ask her some questions.

Barbara had happened upon a ruby and amethyst Boivin

starfish in the Marché aux Puces in northern Paris, where permanent stalls house the flea market that is something of a French institution. As Rebecca Scherm wrote in her novel *Unbecoming*, which describes the Marché, "it was perhaps the only flea market in the world where a six-thousand-euro Louis XIV love seat sat outside on the sidewalk." Barbara prowled the market when she was studying in Paris. She took immediate note of the starfish the day she saw it. "It made me gasp, it was so beautiful," she said. She asked its price of the old woman who was selling it, and remembered, "It was a lot. Probably fifty thousand francs, even then." The old woman in the tiny enclosure eyed her thoughtfully. "Who is buying this?" Barbara asked her. "Americans," was the answer. The woman explained that the starfish had been made by a small French maker for the *haute bourgeoise* Frenchwoman. "She said it was a little intellectual, and it was collected by Americans. I was so intrigued," Barbara said. I was intrigued, too, wondering if Claudette Colbert's lost starfish could have washed up in a flea market stall some forty years after it went missing.

I asked Barbara a variant of the same question that she had asked the old woman in the market: why do women buy starfish? Her answer was thoughtful, as though she had arrived at it over many years as a jeweler. "Buying them is the most perfect escapism. It is just you and a whimsy. There is not enough whimsy in lives today. It's a sea creature! The moment you buy it is a pure moment of definite whimsy for those who can afford it. You can't put a price on the experience."

I found myself thinking about this every time I came close to an owner of the starfish, and I began to understand why some owners wouldn't talk about their starfish. The thrill was in the secrecy, the private moment of owning the piece and putting it on at will. It was a little like a love affair. To go too wide with it, too public, was to diminish the thrill. It was difficult for the owners to explain, some magic alchemy of glee and greed that, I suppose, is not something most of us want to own up to. *Mine.* That was what Ann Marie Stanton remembered about watching Oprah Winfrey at the Oscars one year when a reporter inquired about a piece of jewelry on her dress. "Whose is that?" the reporter asked, expecting Winfrey to name the jeweler who had loaned it. "Mine," said Oprah, taking everyone aback.

It was a Christie's attendant who was showing me a starfish, in a preview to its sale, who distilled the matter down to its essence. She was girlish, lightly slipping the starfish back into its case. "Don't you wish these pieces could talk?" she asked. Yes. Yes, I did.

Chapter Twenty-one

MURRAY MONDSCHEIN, WHOSE NAME LOOMS over the jewelry world, continued to be a presence lurking in the shadows at every turn of my path pursuing the starfishs' story. Ward Landrigan had made the association first. Françoise Cailles in Paris mentioned Murray as someone who knew about the starfish. Susan Abeles of Bonhams recalled walking past Murray's store and seeing one in the window years earlier. Ralph Esmerian, whose relationship with Murray was no doubt complicated, kept urging me to explore Murray's role. Murray had sold Fred Leighton jewelry to Ralph a year after the business pleaded guilty to tax fraud for failing to collect tax on millions of dollars of jewelry. Murray remained a legend in the trade for reasons other than simply being the face of Fred Leighton over more than thirty years. A Bronx cabdriver's son, he began selling vintage jewelry to accessorize the Mexican wedding dresses and crafts that he sold in Greenwich Village in the late seventies. Obviously a man with a Midas touch, he began to operate under the name Fred Leighton and became the go-to jeweler for one-of-a-kind estate jewelry pieces in his awninged corner store on Madison Avenue and Sixty-sixth Street until he sold it to Esmerian in 2006. Fred Leighton jewelers carried all the great designers from Van Cleef and Tiffany to Belperron and Boivin. In the 1990s, according to Pat Saling, Murray made some starfish for Asprey, the British jeweler who bought the Boivin brand in 1991. Through Pat as his spokesperson he told me repeatedly that he is no longer in the business, but like a true devotee, he attends almost all the major jewelry shows and auctions in the United States and Europe. He is both an elusive and peripatetic character. King of the hill, he needs no publicity.

I learned of Murray's significance in the jewelry world and in the starfishs' story mostly through other jewelers. Mark Emanuel, co-owner of David Webb, explained that Murray had trailblazed the "secondary market," estate jewelry. "He monetized estate jewelry. That's the essence of Fred Leighton. . . . Every great piece of jewelry passed through Murray's hands. He figured it out. He was a true merchant. Murray saw everything and he owned everything." He also owned starfish, both early and "later versions," a euphemistic way of saying real and imitation ones.

The starfish Murray made were licensed from Asprey, the British company that bought the Boivin company in 1991, and bore the Boivin brand, but they were considered different from the originals. Slightly bigger and bolder, they did not bear the look of seamless old-world craftsmanship apparent in the originals, jewelers who had seen them told me. I would soon have the opportunity to see for myself. Yet even without comparing the two, it was easy to see why the newer starfish made it difficult to know and to track the exact number of starfish in existence. The originals and the "later ones" tended to be grouped together.

The semantics for these other starfish had become troubling. When I first called them reproductions, Pat Saling bit my head off. Mark Emanuel at David Webb, whom Saling called a reproduction company, reprimanded me further. "The word is negative. Cut it out of your vocabulary. It's a meaningless term. A dirty word," Emanuel had told me and marched me upstairs to the fourth floor of the company's Madison Avenue headquarters to see the workshop where twenty-five master jewelers fabricated David Webb designs. Signed and numbered, they weren't, in his lexicon, reproductions. Yet the ethics of making new versions from old designs still confused me, especially if they bore the name of the original maker, as Murray's did. Among some jewelers there seemed to be an intent to create confusion, if not outright fakery. Of course, the new starfish I had heard of had been made by the Boivin company, albeit without any of the Boivin principals and owned at the time by Prince Jefri Bolkiah, brother of the Sultan of Brunei. They were the "later" or "newer" ones. Ironically, I felt certain that they were signed or stamped R. BOIVIN. The same ethical questions arose about those produced by the Pierre Bergé auction house in Paris with the designs owned by Nathalie Hocq, current owner of the Boivin brand. The drawing I had seen was for a sapphire and emerald starfish, not ruby and amethyst, but it was clearly being marketed as a Boivin item. I suppose technically it was Boivin, on one hand, but I also stubbornly felt that if it wasn't one of the original ruby and amethyst starfish brooches drawn on Moutard's sketchpad and overseen by Madame Boivin, it wasn't one of the ones, be they three or five, that I was seeking. It was a reproduction.

In 2006 a ruby and amethyst starfish owned by Oscar de la Renta's wife Annette came up for auction at Christie's in New York. The lot description said that it was "circa 1935" and bore the "maker's mark for René Boivin." It was priced well below the earlier Boivin ones. The record shows it was "unsold." I have been told by jewelers that it had first been touted by Christie's as an original but then it was taken off the market before the sale. However, four years later it was auctioned in the Geneva sale. This time it was described as a 1960s version "in pink leather René Boivin case signed and with maker's mark for René Boivin." When I shared this little tidbit with my husband he commented it was a bit like the automakers' practice of selling new cars by touting the cupholders.

I would later learn of a woman who worked as a model maker in the Boivin atelier in the 1980s and 1990s. Caroline Tappou, in Paris. "At that time we made the models in elastomer," a rubbery polymer product, both viscous and elastic, put over a metal mold, she explained, confirming that there had been starfish credited as Boivin that were not the old originals. This different technique sounded likely to account for the slightly coarser appearance and feel of the "later" versions I had seen. It would rule out the exacting handcrafting and thus save time and money. But something, some je ne sais quoi, was surely lost in the process.

Certain starfish of undetermined vintage have surfaced in other places where it is hard to follow. The late television gossip columnist Claudia Cohen reportedly had a starfish. A society woman who frequented media social events in the 1980s and 1990s tells me she saw Cohen wear it at a party for the legendary *Cosmopolitan* editor-in-chief Helen Gurley Brown in the Rainbow Room restaurant atop Rockefeller Center. Cohen was then married to billionaire Ron Perelman, known for his jewelry taste and collection. His wife after Cohen, the actress Ellen Barkin, amassed a serious collection of fine jewelry that she spoke publicly about selling after their divorce. Pat Saling said that the Cohen starfish came from her and Murray Mondschein. Everything about Cohen, who died of ovarian cancer in 2007, is difficult to track since her estate has been held up in a rancorous family dispute among her daughter Samantha, ex-husband Perelman, and his former in-laws. With $68 million in court costs, nobody has time to discuss a mere piece of jewelry.

Jewelry shows function as watering holes for that rarefied breed of men and women whom I was learning to identify: jewelry dealers. In fact, their lives, when you try to make an appointment with them, seem to be an endless merry-go-round of shows in New York, London, Maastricht, Tucson, Miami, Las Vegas, and on and on. They show their wares to the buying public, but perhaps more important, they advertise what they've got, like plumage, to other jewelers. They buy from each other for their clients and they gossip.

The Haughton International Fine Art & Antique Dealers Show at the Park Avenue Armory in New York has been a leading jewelry marketplace since it began in 1989. I went specifically to meet Stephen Burton, the managing director of Hancocks in London who had been too busy with preparations for the Masterpiece London show to see me the previous spring. Burton had first been mentioned to me by Henry Baker as one of the jewelers likely to see a starfish or any other piece of fine vintage jewelry that arrived in London. When I got there a man in a black raincoat with a stringy ponytail comb-over covering his bald spots was getting all the attention from the attendants behind the counter. Once the man in the raincoat moved on, Burton was free to talk.

He and I sat down at a little table off to the side of his counter. He had given some thought to my queries about the starfish and spoke of Millicent Rogers's, which he had seen when it moved through London with Henry Baker as "the one that got away. I didn't quite buy that," he told me in his lilting British accent. Like other jewelers he is acutely aware of Françoise Cailles's position as sole authenticator of Boivin. "I think she has a full copy of the archives and designs of Boivin," he said. The monopoly, he explained, allows her to charge to authenticate Boivin pieces, and also knocks any middlemen out of the process.

As I put my notes away I told him that I was hoping to find Murray Mondschein at the jewelry show if he was there, but I didn't know what he looked like. "He was just here," he said excitedly, "the man in the black raincoat." I needed to get moving to run him down.

When I passed the booth belonging to A La Vieille Russie, I stopped to talk to Peter Schaffer. Peter, a director of his family's multigenerational business founded in Kiev in the 1850s, is a specialist in the jewelry of the czars. He and his family had always had a special relationship with Millicent Rogers. It was a slow moment on the floor of the fair and Peter sat almost clownishly on a stool, gazing across the aisle and looking to me a bit like Humpty Dumpty about to fall. I asked if he'd seen Murray Mondschein. "He's here," he said. "With his daughter. That way," and he pointed rather matter-of-factly toward the dining area.

I spotted Murray and his daughter having lunch at the back of the dining space. For a while I stood to the side and observed him. He was nothing at all like the dapper image that the name Fred Leighton had conjured up in my imagination. He wore black-and-white suspenders and had a big belly. A stream of younger merchants came up and spoke to him. He was jovial and seemed to enjoy their homage.

Murray and his daughter finished their lunch and took seats in a booth belonging to a beautiful Belgian jewelry designer, Véronique Bamps. Bamps, I had been told by an employee of Bonhams, might know something about the starfish. Murray seemed to be telling her stories. I'd heard he was a talented raconteur. He had been in the business for a long time, and had a lot of yarns to tell. I kept an eye on Murray and his daughter until they rose to leave. I followed him into the aisle and stopped him to introduce myself. Since he had broken two previous appointments with me, I watched to see if he recognized my name. He showed no sign. I explained that I was still anxious to speak with him. "Call Pat. She does my scheduling," he said, moving on. When I called Pat a few hours later, she grew exasperated. "I'm not his secretary," she snapped. I already understood that Murray Mondschein had no intention of talking to me about the starfish.

Time, and goodwill, were obviously running out for my quest. Almost everyone (except for Murray) had been willing to help me the first time around. But now that I knew what the important questions were—the ones whose answers would violate the jewelers' *omertà*—it was no longer a good idea to play along with me. At first, they had patronized me and my quixotic project. Now I was "pushy."

I was at a stalemate with Françoise Cailles. I had e-mailed Françoise several times after our meeting in Paris. In one message I asked if she had ever owned a starfish, as I had been told she had when I made the rounds with London jewelers. It made perfect sense since several jewelers, Lee Siegelson among them, remembered when there had been a starfish in her husband's antiques store. But Cailles did not reply. Several months later I received an e-mail message from Pierre Callies, spelled differently than Cailles. In an attachment was a letter from Françoise with a dateline from Minneapolis.

Dear Ms. Burns,
    I do not know if I received all your mails. I left some of your mail unanswered as result of a busy schedule. Yet, I told you everything I

knew, or everything I could tell you about the starfishes. Neither my
husband nor I can reveal or publish clients' information that is strictly
confidential. This is legal requirement of our professions.

The mention of a legal prohibition against talking about jewelry in Cailles's message was pretty questionable. Granted, there is a convention of confidentiality among dealers that serves them well. And without being specific, she had swiftly dodged my question about owning a starfish. Though she invoked the dealers' claim of confidentiality, the questions I asked her—whether any starfish had been made by Boivin with four instead of six cabochon rubies running down their rays as Susan's did—seemed appropriate to ask the keeper of the standards and history of the House of Boivin. Yet in her view there was no obligation to share them with the world at large. There was certainly no professional requirement for her to cooperate with me, and she had obviously decided, after a nice Paris lunch, to turn me away. I wondered: to what end did she keep her secrets?

A letter that I sent to her husband, Michel Perinet, at their home address asking about his history with the starfish in his store went unanswered. It was clear that they were cutting me off. Nathalie Hocq, who now owned the brand and had bothered to register Boivin Fondation with a domain Internet address in 2012, was taking the same position. She wouldn't speak about it. Boivin and the Boivin starfish were quite literally their business, and they had decided to go into protection mode. Even Lee Seigelson said he didn't want to talk to me anymore about starfish.

After the Haughton show at the Armory, I stopped into Christie's to take in the Important Jewels auction being held there that week. I wanted to watch Rahul Kadakia, the thirty-nine-year-old international head of Christie's Jewelry, run it. Kadakia had been considered a rainmaker in the world of international fine jewelry auctions, following in the footsteps of François Curiel. East Indian by birth, he is a small, impeccably dressed man. Wearing red socks with his tassel loafers, he took his place behind the auction lectern. I sat near the back and watched the crowd. The buyers were mostly men and many wore yarmulkes and fedoras. It seemed everyone had a five o'clock shadow. There were a few women in fur coats, high heels, and sunglasses on such a gray day. Rahul was supremely composed, coaxing bidders and on occasion making light banter with them. There was something polished and princely about him. He had smooth, delicate-looking hands but wielded the auction gavel like he meant it. During a pause between lots I looked over to the rectangular glass jewelry case where some items for the upcoming Magnificent Jewelry sale, some months off, were already displayed. Something caught my eye. I went over for a closer look. There in the middle of the case were two large starfish brooches, one ruby and amethyst, the other emerald and aquamarine! I went back to look more closely. They were bigger and brighter than the ones I had seen so far. I hoped it was just the bright overhead lighting that made them seem so ostentatious and bold, even a little bit gross. I was taken aback. I had doubts that these were originals.

The next morning I was back at Christie's. The room for the previous night's auction was cleared and empty, including the jewelry case where the starfish had been. I wondered if I'd dreamed seeing the starfish at all. I asked in several offices where I could find them. They were gone, I was told. As I had found after the Verdura party, starfish had a way of vanishing overnight. I tried again, more insistently, in another office, where buyers claim their merchandise. The clerk on duty telephoned the jewelry department. They would be available for preview in about six weeks, I was told. I could not see them now. Like sea creatures that slip from sight, the starfish went missing again. Just like that.

Several days before the Magnificent Jewels auction I interviewed Rahul Kadakia. He was out of the office when I was ushered in by an assistant but the starfish were in a purple tray on his desk. I studied them until he arrived. When Rahul came in he held the starfish up and turned it over. Its rays hung limply, reminding me of a bullfrog when he lifted it. It was fully articulated. A phone call interrupted and he excused himself for a moment from the office. "Please," he said, handing the starfish over to me to hold. I was no longer hesitant. I picked up the ruby and amethyst one and took it over to the window to examine it in the light. Its second and fourth rays were upturned at their end. One small amethyst came loose and tumbled to his desk. I wondered if that was the effect I had on these starfish since a similar thing had happened at Nancy Marks's. I placed it in the purple tray. I turned the starfish over but could not make out the tiny maker's marks on its back that might prove its provenance. They were too small to see with a naked eye. When Rahul returned he called an assistant to bring a small plastic bag for the loose amethyst.

He picked the starfish up with far less reverence than I had. With the help of his jeweler's loupe, he studied the marks on its underside. He believed he could make out a palm tree on a stem, the symbol of a fabricator that neither he nor I could identify. Charles Profillet was the fabricator of the original starfish and he usually signed his work. His name was not there. The emerald and aquamarine version had an eagle eye and "Boivin" in block letters, he said. I could not even see them with a magnifying glass. He shrugged. I would need to check out the marks to see what fabricators they signified. He could not, I knew, discuss who had consigned these starfish with Christie's. "These rubies are too purple to be pigeon blood," he said, referring to the fine rubies that were often used by Boivin in the thirties and forties. It sounded as if he was giving me a clue that these starfish were not originals. The catalogue for the collection did not specify that these starfish were made in the 1960s. I could not distinguish the later from the newer starfish by the glossy photos of them in the catalogue, but it was easy to do when you were in their presence or had one in your hand. I'd been told that in one case Françoise Cailles had known the same problem and had authenticated a Boivin piece that she had to recant later after she saw it in person. The originals seemed denser and somehow tighter. It was difficult to explain the difference, and perhaps that intangible je ne sais quoi that dealers spoke of, the scent and spirit of former owners that they believed clung to pieces of estate jewelry, made a difference. Who was I to quibble? A trained expert might have attributed the subtle differences to the workmanship expressed in the goldsmithing, the fitting of the joints, and the setting of the stones. Whatever accounted for the difference, these starfish did not capture one's imagination or make you feel that you held something extraordinary in your hand. I could feel it, but I couldn't quite explain it, just as Janet Zapata had told me I would.

Rahul plopped the starfish into the box.

We began by discussing buyers for the starfish and the brooches' special appeal. "Some [people] prefer diamonds to colored stones but this is an iconic piece," he said, nodding to the starfish on his desk. "It is special. People gravitate to it. It is a very sophisticated piece for some customers who can play with jewelry." He had an idea that the starfish buyer was someone "who has a Harry Winston big diamond. Cartier sapphire earrings. A JAR. Pearls by Mikimoto. Everything that you could possibly want. The Boivin starfish brooch is for a princess or actress. It is fun jewelry, like that gold chain from that summer in the seventies." He called them "big stars" rather than starfish and said that in

his whole career so far he had not seen ten of them, counting the
starfish in different gemstone combinations and sizes. He told me
a story centered on Cartier's tutti-frutti bracelet. It was made of
stones in many different colors. "Why?" he asked rhetorically. "All
the stones from Burma and elsewhere had to go to India for cutting. India would offload its poor-quality gemstones first. 'You
must buy this before we connect you with the maharajah you want
to buy from,' was what they said. So the stones were all polished
in Jaipur. They were carved in Paris." The "tutti-frutti" design
by Cartier from the early 1900s that entailed mixing brightly colored gemstones, typically sapphires, rubies, and emeralds, and putting them in platinum and diamond settings, became a classic
hit. In 2014 a tutti-frutti bracelet sold for $2.1 million at Sothe-
by's. The heiress Daisy Fellowes bought a necklace in 1936, about
the same time that Claudette Colbert bought her Boivin starfish.
"Tutti-frutti was a great example of creativity triumphing over
gems alone," said Rahul, admiring how something of great value
could be made from inferior-quality stones. The same could
be said of Boivin's starfish and other oversized sea creatures whose
value rested on imaginative design rather than the worth of the
stones. The stones that now cost $1,500 to $2,000 a carat were worth
$50 to $100 in the 1930s when Juliette Moutard made the starfish,
guessed Rahul.

Yet he confessed that he was not especially interested in who
owned jewelry. "I always want to know the age and condition of
a piece. It is more important than who owned it." He had the
smooth facial features of a boy, but he talked like a sage. And a
businessman.

The day before the Magnificent Jewels auction that would include
the two starfish, one ruby and amethyst and the other emerald
and aquamarine, I went to Christie's to preview them. They were
laid out with all the other pieces to be auctioned in a viewing

gallery on the ground floor. I browsed around until I saw the
starfish. When I walked up to the counter and was about to ask
the attendant to hand me the starfish a tall man in dark-framed
glasses with a curly ponytail beat me to it. He turned it over briskly
and handed it back. I asked him if he knew about the starfish. In
a British accent he said he'd handled three or four of them before.
I immediately perked up and told him why I was interested. We
chatted for a moment. He was Adam Zebrak, a dealer from Monte
Carlo for SJ Phillips, the firm where I had interviewed the principals in London. I remembered Jonathan Norton and his brother
telling me that they had never seen a starfish and knew nothing
about them. Zebrak was moving fast, previewing many of the
pieces in the room, and I could tell that this starfish was not of
any special interest to him.

The auction the following day was curiously routine. There
were 350 lots to sell and the two starfish were lots 191 and 192,
titled "Property from a distinguished collection" in the catalogue. There was no mention of Françoise Cailles or her authentication, yet the pieces were signed René Boivin, according to the
catalogue. I thought of François Curiel's modernization of the auction world and penchant for marketing when I opened the glossy
four-color catalogue to a photo of the two starfish, the ruby and
amethyst one in front, the emerald and aquamarine one in back.
They were posed standing on tips like two dancers with their arms
spread in a pas de deux or cartwheel for a full page. Images of the
pieces for sale flashed up on a big projection screen above the
auctioneer during the bidding. Things had come a long way from
the time when jewelry was laid out in gray cardboard boxes and
looked all the same.

The starfish did not come up for several hours into the bidding. Then they came and went in a blink without much competition. The catalogue estimate had been $80,000 to $120,000 but
the ruby and amethyst starfish actually sold for $137,000, the

emerald and aquamarine one for $125,000. While these numbers topped the estimates, it was clear that the audience knew, as did I, that these starfish were not Boivin originals. A JAR diamond flower cuff bracelet in the next lot was listed for $600,000 to $800,000.

There was no way to know who the buyer of the starfish was and whether he or she was seated in the room or on the other end of the telephone line. As I left the room, Adam Zebrak stood nearby. I had seen him seated next to Murray Mondschein, who was wearing black-and-white suspenders patterned with skulls and crossbones, a few rows in front of me. "Murray said that it wasn't one he'd made," he told me. I was surprised that he shared this confidence with me. It was significant that he spoke at all of starfish that Murray had made. If not Murray, who then? I wondered. Maybe Nathalie Hocq and Pierre Bergé or their former colleague in the auction world, Frédéric Chambre? I remembered that Ann Ziff had said that she had seen a starfish at auction on the second floor of the PBA house in Paris.

After the auction I located Adam Zebrak through SJ Phillips in London and asked him to tell me about the starfish that he had handled. He wrote back, "I have owned a couple over the years and have sold them to Fred Leighton. I do not discuss my clients, customers, or past glories. Privacy is my policy...!!" Obviously, I was learning, Fred Leighton, aka Murray Mondschein, was a strand upon which many starfish had washed ashore, and some were even spawned there.

Ralph Esmerian, the dapper fourth-generation jeweler who bought the Fred Leighton jewelry company from the retiring Murray Mondschein in 2006, remembered, "Murray Mondschein (better known by his name change to Fred Leighton) proudly showed me a couple of starfish in the 1980s that he had commissioned the Boivin firm to make for him." I wondered, was it the

1980s or the 1990s that Pat Saling mentioned, but I had learned by talking to jewelers that there was some fluid margin for accuracy, even if it rattled my journalistic nerves. Ralph continued, "I voiced my objections to such copies, expressing (and knowing him) that within a few years such reproductions would be represented as originals from the 30s and 40s." Ralph corresponded with me by letter while he served his time in the Canaan federal prison in Waymart, Pennsylvania. He had become one of my best sources about the starfish and the people who might know something about them. He added, "When Murray bought some of Diana Vreeland's jewelry, I thought he showed me an original Boivin starfish—but I'm not certain." I could find no record of a starfish in Vreeland's estate, yet the starfish would have fit right in with her penchant for things red and big. Her sons directed me to fashion jewelry king Kenneth Jay Lane, who helped Vreeland with her jewelry collection and unabashedly copied Chanel cuffs and other master jewelers' pieces for her, the Duchess of Windsor, Jackie Kennedy, and other stylish women. But he could not recall seeing a Boivin starfish in her costume or fine jewelry collections.

Those "reproductions" that Ralph mentioned had been made during the time that Jacques Bernard owned Boivin and ran its business for Asprey. There was no question any longer in my mind that Murray had made and offered "later" starfish for sale, and there was evidence that an original may have passed through Fred Leighton jewelry at some time, but I wasn't going to learn about it firsthand. I couldn't help wondering if the later ones had been presented for sale as originals. There was at least room for confusion. Of that I was certain.

It was obvious to me that there was money to be made by anyone who produced copies of the original starfish and inserted them into the market. They could count on the guardians of integrity of these works of art to be tolerant of the imitation process.

The question of counterfeits dogged and intrigued me. I grappled with the term since most later starfish were made more or less under Boivin's extended auspices, but I wondered how this differed from a hypothetical example I made up. What if the Ford Motor Company made a copy today of the original Mustang pony model of 1964? It would be very easy to distinguish from the "later" ones made in 2015. Both are called Mustangs, but no fancier of the sixties classic would be satisfied by the modern version, I bet. More to the point, no one would be fooled into believing that the later version was an original. Jewelry is different.

When I heard back from Ann Ziff's office about the sale dates and location of her starfish, I realized her starfish was the one I had handled and seen auctioned at Christie's. "Property from a distinguished collection" was the only hint of its provenance in the catalogue and there was no claim that it, or its emerald and aquamarine partner, had been authenticated by Françoise Cailles or that they had been made in the 1930s. And they had been priced accordingly. By this time I found it only mildly surprising that no one had bothered to point out to me, when I was on hand asking questions, that this ruby and amethyst starfish was not one of those I was looking for, unless I counted Rahul Kadakia's telling comment that the rubies were not of pigeon-blood hue. He had played along while we studied the ruby and amethyst piece, looking for puncheons and signatures. Though signed with the Boivin stamp, which could have been real or added later, it was not one of the original three. It was a later model.

Ziff's starfish were the best example I had encountered so far of how starfish reproductions, no matter what you called them, could crawl into the market and obscure the trail of the originals. Yet, Ziff's appreciation and enjoyment of the pieces did not depend on their authenticity. The starfish's beauty and articulation were satisfying enough for her. They were well made, and indeed, they were technically the Boivin brand. There is always confusion surrounding the signed pieces, since Madame Boivin had maintained that Boivin creations needed no signature to identify them. The assay marks by the fabricators, like Charles Profillet, were one indication of original provenance, but a piece that was out-and-out signed by Boivin was more likely to have been made later by Asprey. It didn't make a lot of sense and felt like a good round of the childhood game of opposites, in which you said everything you didn't mean, or the way that tornadoes and toilets reverse their spins in the southern hemisphere.

It was time to take stock. I had now discovered and held two of the original Boivin starfish in my hands and I knew that Millicent Rogers's was floating around New York City, on the bosom of a Van Cleef & Arpels client who was an aficionada of the arts. Jennifer Tilly had a fine original one in Los Angeles.

Chapter Twenty-two

HEARD ABOUT THE ORIGINAL MIAMI BEACH ANTIQUES AND
Estate Jewelry Fair from Natalie Bos, who writes the Jewels-
DuJour jewelry blog. Bos had featured Boivin starfish on her
blog in the past and I was anxious to speak with her. We met
for coffee.

Bos had never seen a full-sized Boivin ruby and amethyst starfish, though she had devoted a blog entry to a report that Stephen
Russell and Lee Siegelson were showing Rogers's around the dealers' market. When I asked her which of the various jewelry auctions
I should attend in order to familiarize myself with the scene, she
hardly paused before suggesting Miami. I was surprised. I had
expected her to say Maastricht in the Netherlands, or the Masterpieces, or even Baselworld in Basel, Switzerland, which claims it
is the most important and trendsetting show for the watch and

jewelry industry. One hundred fifty thousand people attended that weeklong event in 2015. But the Original Miami Beach Antique Show in January was her suggestion. "They'll all be there," she explained, meaning the dealers I had been hunting and talking to for several years now.

She was right. The Original Miami Beach Antique Show claims to be the world's largest indoor antiques show. Its wares range from Renaissance to Art Deco. A thousand dealers from twenty-eight countries attract twenty thousand attendees to South Florida.

It had begun pouring rain the night before the show and continued into the next day when I arrived through puddles outside the bland, one-story box building of the Miami Beach convention hall. Inside it became obvious that the majority of the shoppers were dealers buying from other dealers. I felt I had landed in territory that was a cross between a fishbowl and a Fellini movie. The windowless space gave no hint of the weather outside, day or night. Inside the air was full of purpose as people consulted their catalogues and moved through the square grid of aisles. This jewelry fair was not a place for carefree shoppers to ooh and ahh over the pretty pieces. It was more like a trade show: serious business for those who attended. The dozen or so dealers I had pursued in New York and Europe were listed in the directory, along with over a hundred wholesalers from Tel Aviv and hundreds from other places. French, Spanish, and Italian were heard as much on the floor as English. I wandered around aimlessly at first, just to get my bearings, and when I looked up, lo and behold, there was Pat Saling in a turquoise blazer behind the counter of her booth. The customer shopping ahead of me was the Belgian dealer Véronique Bamps, wearing moccasins and jeans, and looking, she said, for a certain Cartier bracelet. When Bamps moved on I approached Saling with a couple of follow-up questions about when she had sold jewelry to Imelda Marcos. Her face hardened when she recognized me. I asked if she had heard anything more about the Boivin starfish since I had interviewed her the prior year. She said she hadn't. "I wouldn't tell you if I did know," she added. I asked if Murray was at the convention. "He's here," she said, turning her charm toward another customer.

I milled through aisles of telescopes, Hermès scarves, silverware, vintage crystal, and paintings mixed in the rows, maybe even miles, of jewelry. There was just enough kitsch to offer some relief. I stopped to touch the ears of a full-sized Yoda statue in a booth with jukeboxes and bar toys. They didn't wiggle as I'd hoped.

After almost three years of chasing the starfish and the dealers who handled them, I found this show was a bit like a family reunion, complete with irritable old aunts and uncles, their names displayed behind their booths. I recognized the players in my story and knew better what to ask of them at this stage of the game than when I had first met them. Typically crisp and dressed for business when I'd met them in cities, everyone was a bit rumpled and casual in the Florida humidity. I hoped that would mean more accessible.

I went looking for Martin Travis from Symbolic & Chase, whom I had missed seeing in London. I knew that Martin had sold a diamond starfish brooch a few years earlier in London and he was familiar with Boivin. Sandy-haired and wearing jeans, he was younger than I had imagined.

I passed Russell Zelenetz, wearing a quilted vest with his shirttail hanging out, along the way. We chatted for a second. He told me that Murray Mondschein now moved around in a motorized wheelchair. For a moment I pondered whether that would make him easier or more difficult to corner.

I had better luck with Simon Teakle, the Connecticut jeweler who had formerly worked for Christie's. We had only spoken previously by phone. When I introduced myself to him at his booth he reacted to my mention that I had heard from a former starfish owner, Ann Ziff, that she had first seen one being worn by a woman "who was on the board of the Met." I had taken that to mean the Metropolitan Opera. But a light went off for Simon when I said it. "No, it was the Metropolitan Museum. It had to be Jayne Wrightsman," he crowed. In fact, he had been the auctioneer at Christie's in 1995 when they sold the Wrightsman collection, one of the top ten most expensive private jewelry collections in the world. He remembered the collection and the starfish. I was heartened. The name Wrightsman also rang a bell with me. The Wrightsman wing of American colonial furnishings at the Metropolitan Museum had been a donation from the wealthy oil executive and philanthropists Charles and Jayne Wrightsman. It made perfect sense that such a woman would have had a starfish.

Then I moved along to see Sam Loxton, the only man in sight who was wearing a suit and tie. I told him I had been unable to contact Nathalie Hocq after he had given me her email address two years earlier. I hoped she was at the Miami show. He shook his head. He'd heard that she was in India—Jaipur, the jewel center of India, to be exact. I told him that I was starting to doubt that there were any Boivin archives. "The archive exists," he assured me. The same frustration over Nathalie Hocq and the archives opened up in me again.

Sharing Sam's counter space was a man I had long wanted to meet, Dominik Biehler. Biehler is owner of the Munich-based jewelry and gem merchant Ernst Färber, which claims to have been in business since 1692. We had exchanged a half-dozen e-mails. Biehler, I knew, underwrote Sam Loxton's purchase of the Millicent Rogers starfish and the hippocamp. I had been told that his family connections go way back with Michel Perinet, Françoise Cailles's husband, in Paris, and that in fact, he had been in their wedding party. This reminded me again of what a tight-knit guild jewelers comprised. So it did not come as much of a surprise when he told me that he had first seen a ruby and amethyst Boivin starfish brooch at Michel's store in Paris in 1995. I wondered if it had been the missing third starfish that had stayed in Paris, possibly with the Boivin family or even São Schlumberger. Or even with Françoise Cailles. She had not replied when I asked her outright if she had ever owned a starfish. And of course it was always possible that the starfish in Perinet's was Claudette Colbert's, risen from the depths.

Emmanuelle Chassard, the Paris jeweler who had told me via e-mail that she sold an original starfish in 2012 from her store La Galerie Parisienne, was also there. Her father, Alain, that most wonderful kind of slightly tousled older Frenchman, was manning their booth alongside her. Yes, they once had a starfish, he said. "An exceptional piece from an exceptional French family." I had heard rumors that Emmanuelle was most likely to become the authenticator of Boivin if and when Cailles retired. I had somehow expected a colder, polished Frenchwoman, but Emmanuelle was surprisingly down-to-earth. Wearing little makeup and with her gray-streaked hair hanging loose, she told me that yes, a starfish had sold from her store. She said that she did not know where the starfish had come from. This kind of assertion always amazed me but suggested she had bought it at auction. "I like it to be a mystery. I usually don't want to know because the mystery of the piece adds to their mystique. And sometimes the story is very sad," she said. Ah, I thought, the French, always romantic, always ready to embrace secrecy and discretion. Or, as her countryman André Chervin had explained it to me more pragmatically, "The French are more secretive for a reason. They don't want to attract the attention of the tax man."

Before calling it a day, I stopped to see Adam Zebrak, the jeweler for SJ Norton. I said hello and asked him where he had first seen a starfish brooch. Adam was all smiles and winning ways. "Twenty-five years ago with Murray," he said.

The following day I first noticed Russell Zelenetz and Stephen Feuerman standing in the center of the aisle talking to Zebrak, and then I noticed the motorized chair at their feet. In it was Murray, a bit better groomed than I had seen him before, his hair combed back smoothly, freshly shaven. He sported a Paul & Shark brand white yachting windbreaker. I walked up and reintroduced myself to him. Russell and Stephen disappeared instantly. For some reason I was reminded how, in "'Twas the Night Before Christmas," reindeer scattered like "leaves before the wild hurricane fly."

I explained to Murray that almost everyone I had talked to about the starfish had mentioned him and his connection to them. I was anxious to speak with him. "I have nothing to say," he said flatly. But didn't he want to speak for himself rather than have me write about him from the perspective of others? I asked. I waited a beat until this man, a legend in his trade whom I had pursued now for three years, shook his head and finally spoke. He looked up at me, unsmiling, with eyes as hard as a reptile's. "What's it benefit me?" he asked, revved up his chair, and zipped away. I had my answer, and left town. I never saw Murray again. He died two years later.

I did not learn in Miami who had the Millicent Rogers starfish. It could not be the one that Teakle remembered selling to Jayne Wrightsman in 1995. At that time, Rogers's was still in her daughter-in-law Jackie's possession. Still, I wrote to Wrightsman. Shortly, I heard back from her assistant:

I am sensitive to your request but please know that
Mrs. Wrightsman simply never gives interviews of

```
any nature and to anyone. You are correct in saying
she is a very private person.
```

It seemed oddly appropriate that the e-mail message was written in Courier New typeface, which made me think of an old
typewriter. It was a formal policy from a past era, delivered by
the buffering personal assistant. Ah yes, a *private person*. That was a
claim I had often heard in my reporting life from celebrities just
before they spilled all their secrets, but I could not prevail upon
Mrs. Wrightsman to discuss her former starfish. It would have to
be enough to know that she once had one.

After Miami, a new feeling crept over me. I was near the end of
the starfish's trail. When I sat back and considered them, they
danced before me like a fast-forward newsreel compressing time.
I saw them one by one being swept off the counter of the Boivin
salon in Paris and falling into handbags and carrying trunks. I
knew that a few had cartwheeled with Adam Zebrak through
Monte Carlo. Others had been handed off in paper bags, pig-
skin boxes, and velvet sleeves. Still others, like Millicent Rogers's,
appropriately enough, had basked in the showroom lighting of
Lucas Rarities and traveled with Lee Siegelson to European auctions and shows. It was obvious that at times, they had almost
mimicked real starfish in the way they propagated. Those "later"
versions had multiplied on occasion, slipping into the mix to
make an appearance and confuse matters.

I assumed the story of the Boivin starfish would continue even
when it was over for me. Those brooches that I knew were tucked
into safes and jewelry boxes in Manhattan and Hollywood would
eventually be handed down, sold, or auctioned by a generation to
come. Some of the same dealers would be there ready to ease the
process. I thought that the new owners of the starfish would not
be as colorful or romantic as Claudette Colbert, Millicent Rogers,

São Schlumberger, and others had been, but I couldn't know that for certain.

The whereabouts of Millicent Rogers's brooch nagged me. It was a delicious mystery, the buyer who managed to keep it a secret and the dealers who knew, but shivered in their boots at the prospect of raising the ire of a rich jewelry collector by exposing her. She was probably a lovely person, but in this story she was becoming my wicked queen. Deep Throat had promised to confirm her identity if I discovered her on my own, but he/she would not give me her name.

I wrote Nicholas Luchsinger at Van Cleef in Paris again. He sent his apologies for being unable to help me further, along with the caveat that he knew I understood his position. I did. I touched base with a few of the dealers and sources I hadn't seen in a while to see if they'd learned anything new. Janet Zapata had not heard again from her mystery caller. I went over and over the only leads I had. The owner lived in New York and was involved in the musical arts. She was a "private person." I had never given credence to the idea that she was a singer or actress. While that could be what "musical arts" meant, entertainers usually weren't private people. I ruled out Broadway performers. Rather, I had assumed that it was someone like Ann Ziff, who had served on the board of the Metropolitan Opera. I remembered that Ziff said she had seen a starfish on a Met board member, but it sounded as if it was before the Rogers starfish had left the Rogers family.

I found a list of board members and went down it. Mercedes Bass, I knew, was a wealthy fashionable woman who might have such jewelry, but when I wrote to her assistant in Texas, where she lives, the message came back promptly that she did not have a Boivin ruby and amethyst starfish and did not know of anyone who did. I was acquainted with Daisy Soros, who had been on the board, but I had never seen her wear jewelry of quite the magnitude of the starfish. Still, I asked if she had ever seen a starfish.

She had not. The eleven-person board plus twenty-some managing directors of the Metropoliton Opera seemed a whole cast and chorus. Many names there I didn't know. I paused when I came to the new president, Judith-Ann Corrente. Hers was a name I didn't recognize. I Googled her. Whenever a photo of her came up she was wearing a big gem-studded brooch. Corrente is a very attractive, trim brunette who serves a number of philanthropic interests. I Googled her again, this time with Van Cleef & Arpels in the subject line. There she was, seated and resplendent, wearing ruby earrings and a large circular brooch (presumably from Van Cleef) on a purple suit at the Women's Committee Fall Lunch for the Central Park Conservancy in 2011, sponsored by Van Cleef. She was seated next to Nicholas Luchsinger.

Corrente wore beautiful jewelry in all the photos that flashed up on my computer. Deep Throat had told me that the owner of the Millicent Rogers starfish had jewelry by all the master jewelers, which I took to mean Cartier, Schlumberger, Van Cleef & Arpels, Belperron, and Boucheron. She was a bonafide collector. Olive skinned and long necked, Corrente wore dangling ruby earrings to advantage. In one photo with her husband, Willem Kooyker, head of Blenheim Capital Management, an emerald and diamond aigrette (an elongated ornament that historically served as a plume on tiaras) dangled at her waist. But what convinced me that she was the likely owner of Millicent Rogers's ruby and amethyst starfish brooch was something else. She fit the profile of their owners.

Judith-Ann Corrente was obviously a serious person. She had been one of nine women in the inaugural coed class at Princeton University. She was a dedicated philanthropist and president of the Monteforte Foundation she created with her husband. She was a thinker, exactly the kind of woman that I had learned gravitated to the Boivin starfish. Perhaps it was arguable that São Schlumberger had not been as focused as the other starfish owners, but what she lacked in wits she made up for with style-setting dynamism. None of the starfish owners had been ordinary rich women. They weren't Marie Antoinette, heaping on excess for its own sake.

I fired off a message to Deep Throat but got no reply, which made me think I might be on the right track. I asked another collector if she knew anything about Corrente. She didn't know much except that Corrente had been at a Van Cleef event at the Cooper Hewitt museum in New York in 2011. I wrote a letter to Corrente and sent it to her in care of the Metropolitan Opera. I received no reply. The business office gave me an e-mail address for her. I attached a copy of my original letter. I heard nothing back.

I remembered something that Françoise Cailles had told me in Paris. "The more beautiful the jewelry, the less you see it. Unless you are the kind of person who wants to be seen, like the nouveau riche. When it's beautiful and expensive you don't show it." I could see some of this dynamic at work. Corrente was determined to stay private. A few people who knew her told me that she was reserved, even a bit aloof. One woman described her as severe and added that her husband, Kooyker, is the warmer, more outgoing personality in their partnership. Nobody ever said that conviviality was a requisite for owning a starfish.

Several weeks later I got an e-mail from Deep Throat. "Well done," it read.

Knowing that Corrente had Millicent's starfish gave me a lift I hadn't expected. Of course, I was relieved to have located it, but more than that, Corrente seemed the perfect custodian of the piece. Beautiful, sophisticated, and, I assumed, self-assured, she had had many occasions where she could discreetly have worn a Boivin ruby and amethyst starfish brooch. The Internet was flooded with photos of her on opening nights at the Metropolitan Opera. She had not worn the starfish in the photos I saw, but she seemed a woman who moved in many ways and along the same vein as Millicent Rogers had—Corrente wore a stunning black-and-white Schiaparelli dress to the opening of *Otello* in 2015. Corrente was statuesque. All this made me strangely happy.

I did not expect to ever see a Boivin ruby and amethyst starfish again. They had danced through my head and pulled me into their worlds as inexorably as sea sirens had called to sailors in the *Odyssey*. I had followed them into their worlds and was satisfied that I could get no closer without abandoning reason altogether. I would slip away from the jewelry world now.

I had known when I began my starfish quest that there were likely to be mysteries I could not solve. I had expected the final owner of Millicent Rogers's starfish, so carefully guarded by the jewelry world, to be the unsolved puzzle in the story. But in fact, it was Claudette Colbert's first starfish that I could not identify. Lost? Stolen? Misplaced? It had clearly been to the underside and back, but I suspected that it had re-emerged from the dark as one of the four I had seen.

Had it been the one on São Schlumberger's mink coat on the way to Malcom Forbes's party? Did it live in Nancy Marks's Central Park South penthouse or Susan Rotenstreich's Park Avenue apartment? Was it locked in a safe in Paris, bound to reappear at some later auction? I could not know. But I felt sure that, like all fine jewelry with a world of hunters keeping an eye out for it, it would surface again. While my story had ended, the starfish's would continue, and they would continue to move through the secret sands of wealth, commerce, and beauty until a time when such things were no longer sought or mattered. Meanwhile, even though I tried to leave the starfish's story behind, it sometimes surfaced in my mind, as if in a dream.

In that dream I stand before Boivin's last address at 4 Avenue de l'Opéra. The graceful stone arch over two-story wooden doors still stands proud and grand, but the street below the former upstairs salon is now lined with the shiny façades of modern commerce. I walk right through those twenty-first-century stone walls as if they were illusions and climb the stairs to the cobwebbed workshop with sturdy benches and drawing boards lighted by high windows. It is intensely nostalgic, although I have never been there. Yet it is lifeless. The magic of the bygone era that incubated the starfish is missing. The Buddha sculpture at the salon's entrance is gone. There are no pencils or paint sets on the tabletops, no molds to which the supple starfish arms were shaped, no metal shavings gleaned from the gold settings or sparkling flakes chipped from jewels. The play of wondrous imaginations and imperious demands for perfection that brought the starfish to life are dissipated. All that is left, as I stare around the dusty salon, is a faint but unmistakable whiff of salt, the tang of the beaches of Brittany.

Acknowledgments

It takes many generous people to amass the details of a time gone by. In the case of three pieces of famous French jewelry lost in a world of total discretion, it took an army. I am especially appreciative of those experts in the jewelry world who tutored me in its workings and pointed me on my way: Claudine Seroussi, Audrey Friedman, Ralph Esmerian, Ward Landrigan, Caroline Stetson, Lee Siegelson, Sarah Davis, Janet Zapata, Susan Abelas, Françoise Cailles, Russell Zelenetz, Stephen Feuerman, Pat Saling, Mark Emanuel, Marie-Caroline de Brosses, Sam Loxton, Dominik Biehler, Henry Baker, Nicholas Luchsinger, André Chervin, Sylvain Chervin, James Givenchy, Simon Teakle, François Curiel, Christopher Walling, Barbara Harris, Ann Marie Stanton, Daphne Lingon, Natalie Bos, Peter Edwards, Francesca Amfitheatrof, Rahul Kadakia, Ulysses Grant Dietz, Geoffrey Munn, Evelynne Possémé, Emmanuelle Chassard, and Martin Travis.

I greatly appreciated those who racked their brains to remember anything about the starfish or their owners: Bob and Helen Bernstein, Helen O'Hagan, Elizabeth Bray Irvine, the late Robert Hatfield Ellsworth, and Vivienne Becker. A special thanks to Colleen Caslin, for loaning me a jewelry book that I held on to for five years. I am grateful to the jewelry fanciers and collectors who told me their stories: Susan Rotenstreich, Nancy Marks, Susan Tennenbaum, Lorian Buckley, the late Jackie Peralta-Ramos, Jennifer

Tilly, Ann Ziff, and Pamela Lipkin. Thank you to Jan Reeder and Stephane André, who were quick to make introductions for me, and to Landt Dennis, Sophie Lenoir, and Alain Pinto, who helped me correspond in French without humiliation (that I am aware of). I am grateful to Betty Kojic, who prods to make things happen.

I must especially thank Olivier Baroin and Jean-Pierre Brun, who responded graciously, generously, and promptly to my endless follow-up questions about Boivin in the 1930s. Phil Poirier in Taos and Caroline Tappou in Paris answered tedious queries about the way jewelry was crafted more than eighty years ago.

I owe much to my agent, Cynthia Cannell, for her support of a different concept, to St. Martin's Press for letting me go "fishing," and to my editor, Michael Flamini, for his deft touch and vision. Vicki Lame and Gwen Hawkes kept us on track and schedule. Ragnhild Hagen saved me from woe.

I count on my daughter, Jessie Duncan, for honest feedback, and as always I must thank my husband, Dick Duncan, who keeps me on the journalistic straight and narrow and picks me up when I stumble.

Notes

Chapter 4

1. Vivienne Becker, author of *The Impossible Collection of Jewelry* (New York, Assouline 2013). Interview with author.

Chapter 5

1. Françoise Cailles, *René Boivin: Jeweller* (London, Quartet Books, 1994), p. 6.
2. Ibid, p. 11.
3. Roger Shattuck, *The Banquet Years* (New York, Vintage Books, 1968), p. 5.
4. Nazanin Lankarani, "An Unsigned Iconoclast of 20th Century Design," *New York Times,* December 10, 2010.
5. David Bennett and Daniela Mascetti, *Understanding Jewellery* (Woodbridge, Suffolk, England, Antique Collectors' Club Ltd., 1989), p. 251.
6. Cailles, p. 37.

Chapter 7

1. Cailles, p. 58.
2. Ibid, p. 68.
3. Ibid, p. 56.
4. Ibid, p. 85.
5. https://en.wikipedia.org/wiki/Le_Chabanais

Chapter 8

1. In fact, it was 2006.

Chapter 10

1. Bennet and Mascetti, *Understanding Jewellery,* p. 251.

Chapter 19

1. Sam Loxton, foreword to *No Stone Unturned* by Claudine Seroussi
   Bretagne (Lucas Parities, London, 2012).
2. The Swiss franc and U.S. dollar were close in value.

Index

A

Abdallah, Naguib, 178
Abeles, Susan
  Berj Zavian and, 69–70
  Jennifer Tilly's starfish and,
    171
  jewelers as wolves and, 150,
    161
  Murray Mondschein and,
    186
aigrette, 211
Alexandra (Queen of
    England), 26
amethysts, 22, 49, 70, 100
Antiques Roadshow, 66
aquamarine and emerald
    starfish, 163, 182–183,
    194–195, 197–199, 201
archives (Belperron), 101,
    150–151
archives (Boivin)
  authentication and, 137, 191
  existence of, 206

Nathalie Hocq and, 164–167
  ownership of, 137
  sales records, design orders
    and, 139
  secrecy and, 46, 137
Argyll (Duchess of), 158–159
art, comparison of jewelry to,
    42
Art Deco, 43, 46, 120
Art Loss Register, 158–159
Art Nouveau, 29–30
articulated jewelry, popularity
    of, 95
articulated rays
  description of, 19
  as distinguishing features,
    79–80
  Juliette Moutard and,
    49–50
  reproductions and, 195
  of Rogers' starfish, 100, 112
  Susan Rotenstreich and, 77
Artifacts (website), 74

Asprey, 187

assay marks

authentication and, 54,
127–129

confusion over, 202

later addition of, 145–146

on later starfish, 195

rationale for lack of, 45

Susan Rotenstreich's
starfish and, 79–80, 83

attachment, 57

auction houses, 72

authentication

assay marks and, 54, 127–129

Boivin archives and, 137, 191

Francoise Cailles and,
127–128, 131, 137–138,
190–191

importance of, 40

valuation and, 137–138

avant-garde, 26

B

baguettes, 100, 104–105

Baker, Henry

Jackie Ramos and, 110–117

Millicent Rogers' starfish
and, 110–117, 119–120, 122,
123, 190

Baker, Josephine, 95

Balcom, Ronnie, 100, 103

Bamps, Véronique, 191–192,
204

Barkin, Ellen, 189

Baroin, Olivier, 46, 150–152,
166

Bass, Mercedes, 210

Becker, Vivienne, 18–19, 120

Belle Epoque, 26

Belperron, Suzanne

archives of, 101, 150–152

description of, 48, 134

starfish of, 136–137

success of, 95

work of, 44–46

belt buckle, 107, 180–181

Bentley & Skinner, 124–125

Bergé, Pierre, 147, 165–166

Bernard, Jacques, 63, 142, 164,
200

Bernhardt, Sarah, 102

Bernstein, Bob and Helen,
91–92

bestiaries, 29

Biehler, Dominik, 120, 122,
206–207

Bismarck, Mona, 94

blood, identification by, 115,
121

Boivin, Germaine, 49, 135, 164

Boivin, Jeanne

after departure of
Belperron, 46–50

designs of, 43–45

encouragement from, 2

success of, 28–31, 34

Boivin, Pierre, 32

Boivin, René, 27–32, 44

Boivin jewelry salon
  description of, 14
  success of, 28–31, 34
  workmanship, design and,
    21–22

Bolkiah, Jefri, 188

Bonnard, Pierre, 47

Borrusco, Alessandro, 125

Bos, Natalie, 203–204

brands, 145–146

brooches, 29, 33–34, 115

Brown, Helen Gurley, 189

Brun, Jean Pierre, 50–51,
    138–140

Buckley, Lorian, 110–113

Bulgari brooch, 169

Burma, 21

Burton, Richard, 6

Burton, Stephen, 126, 190

butterflies, 95

C

cabochon rubies, 21, 49

Cailles, Françoise
  on attachment, 23
  authentication and, 127–128,
    131, 137–138, 190–191
  on authorship of individual
    pieces, 54
  book written by, 163
  expertise of, 136

lack of help from, 192–193
  meeting with, 140–143
  on role of Boivin, 48
  on starfish sold in
    April 1996, 80

Cailles, Perinet, 142

Callies, Pierre, 192

carats, 51, 64–65

Cartier, 33, 46, 197

Caslin, Colleen, 131

catalogue notes, 127–128

Catherine the Great, 27

cats, 29

Ceylon rubies, 70

Chambre, Frédéric, 164, 166

chameleon pieces, 49, 129, 173,
    182

Chanel, Coco, 94

chasing, 51–52

Chassard, Alain, 179, 207

Chassard, Emanuelle, 98, 173,
    179–180, 207

Chervin, André, 97–100, 207

Chervin, Sylvain, 52

Choay, Nathalie Hocq.
    See Hocq, Nathalie

Christie's, 72–75, 80, 162,
    193–194, 197–199

Cluster Jewelry, 66, 69

Cocteau, Jean, 47

codes, 141, 146–147

Cohen, Abe, 23–24

Cohen, Claudia, 65–66, 189–190

Colbert, Claudette
description of, 86–88
design and, 34–35
Colbert's starfish
final owner of, 177–178
as first one, 14, 56
loss of, 85, 90–91
undetermined fate of,
213–214
Colette (writer), 47
confidentiality, 193. *See also*
Secrecy
Cooper, Diana, 95, 127
copies (newer starfish)
distinguishing, 83–84, 196
elastomer and, 189
licensing and, 116
at Magnificent Jewelry sale,
197–199
Murray Mondschein and,
38–39, 63, 66, 187–188
Nathalie Hocq and, 147,
164, 165–166
rules governing, 98–99, 147
value of, 74, 161–162,
200–201
Corbin, Marie, 88, 89
Corrente, Judith-Ann, 211–212
counterfeits, 201. *See also*
Reproductions
Crawford, Joan, 69, 95, 169
Cummings, Joanne, 80–82, 176
Cummings, Nathan, 81–82

Curiel, Francois, 152–153, 194
czars, jewelry of, 191

D

Dalí, Salvador, 178
David Webb, 187, 188
Davière, Robert, 49
Davis, Sarah, 10, 79
Day, Doris, 69
De Beers, 24
de Brosses, Marie Caroline, 47,
49, 133–137
de la Renta, Annette, 188–189
de la Renta, Oscar, 56, 119, 162,
168, 170
de Vilmorin, Louise, 44
dealers, 190
Deep Throat, 160, 180, 210, 211,
212
description of Boivin starfish, 2
design
importance of, 19–24, 43
process of, 28–29
devant-de-corsages, 33
di Verdura, Fulco, 94, 103
Dietz, Ulysses, 52
Downton Abbey, 125
Duncan, Isadora, 102

E

Edwards, Peter, 126–128
Egyptian tombs, 31
elastomer, 189

Ellsworth, Robert Hatfield, 91,
     92–93
Emanuel, Mark, 187, 188
emerald and aquamarine
     starfish, 163, 182–183,
     194–195, 197–199, 201
emerald and sapphire starfish,
     188
Ernst Färber, 120, 206
Esmerian, Ralph
     Jean Pierre Brun and, 140
     later starfish and, 164
     Murray Mondschein and,
          186, 199–200
     Saõ Schlumberger and, 178
estate jewelry, 187

F
fabrication, 50–53, 95–96
Fellowes, Daisy, 95, 96
Fellowes, Reginald, 49
Feuerman, Stephen, 37, 41–42,
     172, 208. See also Stephen
     Russell jewelry salon
Fisher, Eddie, 169
flamingo brooch, 163
flappers, 33
Flato, Paul, 10, 103
flea market, 184
Fleming, Renée, 182
flowers, 29, 44
Fred Leighton Salon, 61–62,
     186–187, 199

Freud, Sigmund, 28
Friedman, Audrey, 58–60
Friman & Stein, 12

G
Gaynor, Janet, 107
gemstones, 23–24, 30. See also
     Specific gemstones
Givenchy, James, 71–72
gold, working with, 51–52,
     95–96
gratification, 37
Greffulhe (Countess of
     France), 26
Groult, André, 47

H
hallmarks, 145–146
Hancocks, 126, 190
Harris, Barbara, 183–184
Haughton International Fine
     Arts & Antiques Dealers
     Show, 190
Heyman, Oscar, 64, 110
hippocamp brooch, 15, 104, 108,
     111–112, 122–123
Hocq, Nathalie
     brand ownership and,
          139–140, 188
     reproductions and, 147, 164,
          165–166
     secrecy and, 46, 193
Horyn, Cathy, 46

House of Boivin
description of, 14
success of, 28–31, 34
workmanship, design and,
21–22
Hughes, Graham, 129, 172–173

I
identification marks
authentication and, 54,
127–129
confusion over, 202
later addition of, 145–146
on later starfish, 195
rationale for lack of, 45
Susan Rotenstreich's
starfish and, 79–80, 83
Important Jewels auction,
193–194
The Impossible Collection of Jewelry
(Becker), 18
inheritance taxes, 148
inspiration, 44
intrigue, 57
It Happened One Night, 86–87

J
jewelry-making process, 28–29
Josephine (Empress), 26

K
Kadakia, Rahul, 193–194,
195–197, 201

karats, 51
Kojik, Betty, 163
Kooyker, Willem, 211
Krupp diamond, 6
Kwiat, 61

L
Lalique, René, 30
Lambert, Eleanor, 179
Landrigan, Nico, 9, 122
Landrigan, Ward
family jewelry and, 73
jewelry business and, 36–37
Jonathan Norton and, 123
Murray Mondschein
and, 62
Suzanne Tennenbaum and,
163
Verdura party and, 5–6, 9
Lane, Kenneth Jay, 200
Leighton, Fred. *See* Fred
Leighton Salon;
Mondschein, Murray
letters to buyers, 75, 76
Lewis, Coco, 87–88
licensing, 116
Lingdon, Daphne, 23, 72–75
Lipkin, Pamela, 154–155
lost starfish, 85, 90–91
lost wax technique, 52
Lotfinder, 72, 74, 81
Loxton, Sam
Boivin archives and, 166

Claudine Seroussi and, 128
description of, 120–122
at the Original Miami
    Beach Antique Show,
    206
Rogers' starfish and, 64, 115
Lucas Rarities, 14–16, 64,
    120–122
Luchsinger, Nicholas, 148–150,
    180, 210, 211

M
Magnificent Jewelry sale, 194,
    197–199
Manishevitz, Haim, 60
Marché aux Puces, 184
Marcos, Imelda, 65, 204
marks
    authentication and, 54,
        127–129
    confusion over, 202
    later addition of, 145–146
    on later starfish, 195
    rationale for lack of, 45
    Susan Rotenstreich's
        starfish and, 79–80, 83
Marks, Nancy, 127, 130, 155–159,
    176–177
Martens, Maria, 107
master jewelers, 27–28
Metropolitan Museum, 206
Metropolitan Opera board,
    210–211

Miami Beach Antiques and
    Estate Jewelry Fair, 203
mistresses, 94
Modern Jewelry (Hughes),
    172–173
Mondschein, Murray. *See also*
    Fred Leighton Salon
    as Fred Leighton, 42
    importance of, 186–188
    jewelry business and, 148
    lack of availability of, 62,
        191–192
    meeting with, 208
    newer starfish and, 38–39,
        63, 66, 86, 187–188,
        199–200
    tax fraud of, 186
money people, 57, 64
Monteforte Foundation, 211
Moutard, Juliette
    description of, 47–49
    design and, 1–2, 49
    distinguishing starfish of,
        136–137
    Marie-Caroline de Brosses
        and, 134
    secrecy and, 46
Munn, Geoffrey, 124

N
naturalism, 29, 49, 95, 128
necklaces, 77
newer starfish, 56, 66, 187–188

newer starfish (reproductions)
  distinguishing, 83–84, 196
  elastomer and, 189
  licensing and, 116
  at Magnificent Jewelry sale,
      197–199
  Murray Mondschein and,
      38–39, 63, 66, 187–188
  Nathalie Hocq and, 147,
      164, 165–166
  rules governing, 98–99, 147
  value of, 74, 161–162, 200–201
Norton, Jonathan, 123–124, 198
Norton, Nicolas, 123, 198
number of starfish
  assay marks and, 161–162
  author's summary of,
      176–177
  Daphne Lingdon on, 74
  ray position and, 79
  Russell Zelentz on, 38–39
  Stephen Russell on, 85–86

O
O'Hagan, Helen, 88–91, 95
Original Miami Beach
      Antique Show, 204–208

P
Panis Angelicus, 182
Paris, 25–27
Pat Saling company, 62. See also
  Saling, Pat

payment plans, 171
pearls, 23–24
perception, importance of, 24
Perelman, Ron, 66, 189–190
Perinet, Michel, 136, 163, 193
Pierre Bergé auction house,
      147, 165–166, 188
pigeon's blood rubies, 21, 181,
      196, 201
Place Vendôme, 47
platinum, 32
points, 64–65
Poiray, 139
Poiret, Jeanne. See Boivin,
      Jeanne
Poiret, Paul, 30–32, 102
Porter, Cole, 47, 90, 109
Possémé, Evelyne, 144–147,
      167
Primavera Gallery, 58–59
Le Prix des Bijoux (Cailles), 163
Profillet, Charles, 50–53, 145,
      195
provenance, 45–46, 54, 121
public records, 72

R
Ramos, Arturo Peralta,
      105–108, 181
Ramos, Jackie, 105–113
Raphaelite, 48
rays, articulated
  description of, 19

as distinguishing features,
79–80
Juliette Moutard and,
49–50
reproductions and, 195
of Rogers' starfish, 100, 112
Susan Rotenstreich
and, 77
René Boivin: Jeweller (Cailles),
131–132, 173
reproductions (newer starfish)
distinguishing, 83–84, 196
elastomer and, 189
licensing and, 116
at Magnificent Jewelry sale,
197–199
Murray Mondschein and,
38–39, 63, 66, 187–188
Nathalie Hocq and, 147,
164, 165–166
rules governing, 98–99,
147
value of, 74, 161–162,
200–201
retiring of designs, 147
Rogers, Millicent
description of, 101–105
multiple, 106–107
origins of, 97–98
as previous owner, 7
ruby heart brooch of, 10–11
treatment of jewelry by,
13–14

Rogers' starfish
Ann Ziff's starfish as one
of, 180–181
discovery of current owner
of, 210–213
Jayne Wrightsman and, 208
path of, 177
resale of, 149
Saling and, 63–64
as second one made, 56
Stephen Burton on, 190–191
variations in, 100, 104–105
romanticism, 36
Rosenthal, Joel Arthur, 155
Rotenstreich, Jon W., 77
Rotenstreich, Susan, 76–84,
176
rubies, 20–22, 70, 195–196, 201
Rue Chabanais, 53
Russell, Stephen, 12
Rutledge, Richard, 15–16

S
salamander with click tail,
181–182
sales prices
Evelyne Possémé on, 147
Francoise Cailles records of,
140–142
Jennifer Tilly's starfish and,
171
of Millicent Rogers'
starfish, 149

sales prices (*continued*)
  Nancy Marks' starfish and, 156
  Olivier Baroin on, 151–152
  Peter Edwards on, 126
  for Ramos collection, 111
  tripling of, 172
Saling, Pat
  lack of help from, 204–205
  later starfish and, 187, 188, 200
  meeting with, 62–66
salons, 31–32
sapphire and emerald starfish, 188
Satie, Erik, 28, 47
Sautoirs, 33
scent, carrying history in, 24
Schaffer, Peter, 191
Scherm, Rebecca, 184
Schiaparelli, Elsa, 31, 96, 102, 106
Schlumberger, Jean, 128
Schlumberger, Pierre, 178
Schlumberger, São, 178–179, 211
Schlumberger, Victoire, 179
secrecy
  André Chervin and, 98
  Boivin archive and, 46
  Claudine Seroussi and, 15–16
  Daphne Lingdon and, 74–75
  Evelyne Possémé and, 167
  Francoise Cailles and, 141–142, 193

Geoffrey Munn and, 124
Janet Zapata and, 57
Jean Pierre Brun and, 138–139
Olivier Baroin and, 151
Stephen Russell and, 40
thrill of, 184–185
security concerns, 78, 109, 155–156
Seroussi, Claudine
  Arturo Peralta Ramos and, 105
  help from, 128–129
  inquiry from about Rogers' starfish, 14–16
  Sam Loxton and, 115, 122
Sheherazade, 31
shows, 190, 204–208
Siegelson, Lee
  Berj Zavian and, 69
  Henry Baker and, 115–116
  Janet Zapata and, 56
  Jennifer Tilly's starfish and, 171
  lack of availability of, 193
  Rogers' starfish and, 10–13, 19, 122, 149
  Stephen Russell and, 37, 38
Siegelson's, 10–13, 38
signature marks
  authentication and, 54, 127–129

confusion over, 202
later addition of, 145–146
on later starfish, 195
rationale for lack of, 45
Susan Rotenstreich's
    starfish and, 79–80, 83
signet rings, 30
Signoria (Palazzo della), 110
Silk Road (China), 21
Simon Teakle Fine Jewelry,
    72
size of starfish, 6, 19, 56, 77–78,
    83–84
SJ Phillips, 123–124, 198, 208
Soros, Daisy, 210
Stanton, Ann Marie, 167–171,
    173–174
starfish hunters, 42
statement brooches, 34
Stephen Russell jewelry salon,
    37–42, 115, 156, 172
Stetson, Caroline, 62
stock market crash of 1929,
    34
stolen starfish, 85, 90–91
Surroko, Tatiana, 7
Symbolic & Chase, 119, 205

T
Taffin, 71
Tajan, 143
Tappou, Caroline, 189
Tarpas, Joanne, 82

Taylor, Elizabeth, 169
Teakle, Simon, 72, 80, 205–206
Tennenbaum, Suzanne,
    163–164
Tiffany & Co., 69
Tilly, Jennifer, 167–173, 174,
    176–177
Travis, Martin, 119, 205
en tremblant, 29
tutti-frutti design, 40, 197

U
Unbecoming (Scherm), 184
upstairs jewelers, 57

V
valuation
    authentication and, 137–138
    carats, points and, 64–65
    of newer starfish, 74,
        161–162, 200–201
    Saling on, 65
    of vintage jewelry, 19–20
    workmanship, design and,
        19–24, 43
Van Cleef & Arpels, 40,
    147–148, 160, 211
Verdura, 4–8, 38
vintage jewelry, valuation of,
    19–20
von Furstenberg, Diane, 156
von Zadora-Gerlof, Andreas,
    179

Vreeland, Diana
  Maltese cross of, 64
  on Millicent Rogers, 103
  Murray Mondschein and,
    200
  ownership of Boivin pieces
    by, 96, 127
  Paul Poiret and, 31

W
Walling, Christopher, 178–181
Warhol, Andy, 178
Wartski jewelers, 124
Water Jewels, 183
Webb, David, 63, 68–69
whelk brooch, 49
whimsy, 184
Windsor (Duchess of), 47, 82
Wladimir (Grand Duchess of
    Russia), 26
wolves, jewelers as, 150, 161
World War I, 32
Wrightsman, Jayne, 206,
    208–209

Z
Zapata, Janet
  Geoffrey Munn and, 124
  Jennifer Tilly's starfish and,
    173

on later starfish, 196
meeting with, 55–58
Millicent Rogers' starfish
    and, 210
on upstairs money people,
    64
Zavian, Berj, 66–71
Zavian, Robin, 67–68
Zebrak, Adam, 198, 199, 208
Zelenetz, Russell. *See also*
    Stephen Russell jewelry
    salon
  Jennifer Tilly's starfish and,
    172
  meeting with, 37–42
  Murray Mondschein and,
    208
  on number of starfish, 85
  at the Original Miami
    Beach Antique Show,
    205
Ziff, Ann
  meeting with, 181–183
  Pierre Bergé auction house
    and, 165–166, 199
  two starfish of, 180, 181,
    201–202
  woman on board of Met
    and, 206
Ziff, William Jr., 181